Contemporary

WORSHIP

Contemporary
WORSHIP

Edited by
TIM AND JAN WRIGHT

ABINGDON PRESS / NASHVILLE

CONTEMPORARY WORSHIP

Copyright © 1997 by Abingdon Press

This book is printed on acid-free, recycled paper.

Library of Congress Cataloging-in-Publication Data

Contemporary worship / edited by Tim and Jan Wright.
     p. cm.
    Includes bibliographical references and index.
    ISBN 0-687-01544-8 (pbk. : alk. paper)
    1. Public worship.   2. Worship programs.   I. Wright, Tim, 1957– .   II. Wright, Jan, 1956– .
  BV15.C63   1997
264—dc20   96-41867
    CIP

Scripture quotations noted NIV are from the *Holy Bible, New International Version.* Copyright © 1973, 1978, 1984 International Bible Society. Used by permission of Zondervan Publishing House. All rights reserved.

Those noted CEV are from the *Contemporary English Version.* Copyright © American Bible Society 1991, 1992.

Those noted KJV are from the Kings James Version of the Bible.

Permission is granted to purchasers of this book to copy the following pages for planning worship services: pages 47-48, 66, 106, 151.

97 98 99 00 01 02 03 04 05 06 — 10 9 8 7 6 5 4 3 2 1

MANUFACTURED IN THE UNITED STATES OF AMERICA

*To all the courageous leaders and congregations
who are coloring outside the lines
in order to affect their communities
for Jesus Christ*

About the Editors

T im Wright is the executive pastor of Community Church of Joy, an Evangelical Lutheran Church in America congregation in Glendale, Arizona and the Executive Director of the Community Church of Joy Leadership Center. He has written A Community of Joy: How to Create Contemporary Worship *(Abingdon Press)*, Unfinished Evangelism: More Than Getting Them in the Door *(Augsburg Fortress), and is featured in* Reaching the Unchurched, *a video seminar with Walt Kallestad (Augsburg Fortress).*

Jan Wright assists Tim in designing and implementing one of the contemporary worship services at Community Church of Joy. She plays keyboards for the Good News Band in that service. She enjoys teaching classes at church and leading workshops during the church's evangelism conference. She also works as a cast member for The Disney Store. Tim and Jan have two children, Alycia and Mike, along with several birds.

All proceeds from this book go directly to the Community Church of Joy Leadership Center—a center designed to equip pastors and layleaders for effective twenty-first-century ministry.

Contents

Part 3: Contemporary Praise Services

Part 4: Contemporary Outreach-Oriented Services

Introduction

In the 1960s two significant events took place that changed the shape of ministry, perhaps forever:

1. The "De-Churching" of America. During the years before and shortly after World War II, mainstream denominations in the U.S. enjoyed tremendous growth. Throughout that time the church played an important role in the lives of most Americans. Church life was woven into the fabric of the nation. The values of Christianity were respected and adhered to by many. When the church spoke, people listened. Christianity had influence. People and entire families loyally committed themselves to denominations for years and even for generations. Most were enculturated into the church from birth on. If you were a teenager around World War II, 90 percent of your friends would have been churched.

But that all changed in the 1960s. Baby boomers (the generation born between 1946 and 1964) started leaving the church in droves. While 90 percent of them had been churched as children, two-thirds left the fold in their teens and twenties. The church they grew up with ceased to interest them or hold their attention. It no longer spoke their language. The voice of the church was increasingly ignored as irrelevant and out of touch. Institutional and denominational loyalty began to drop. The values of Christianity no longer affected the lifestyles of Americans.

As a result, new generations of people are becoming increasingly secular and illiterate about church culture and speech. If you are a teenager in the mid-1990s, 50 percent of your friends will have some kind of contact with a church. For children born in 1995, only 30 percent of their friends will have been influenced by the church by the time they turn seventeen. That's the "de-churching" of America. Today's generations have no idea what Christians are talking about. Our styles of worship and forms of ministry have become unintelligible.

2. The "Rock 'n' Rolling" of America. With the 1950s to 1960s and the teen years of boomers came a brand new music—rock 'n' roll. While every generation has had its own music, rock 'n' roll was different. It not only shared the values of boomers through its lyrics, but it also shaped those values. It gave boomers a common voice. It rallied them together. It influenced their views on life. More than music, rock 'n' roll became the heart language of the baby boom generation. And its many manifestations in newer generations will function in much the same way.

A New Day of Mission

The outcome of these two events has been the creation of a brand new mission field. As each new generation becomes increasingly unchurched, congregations will have to envision new strategies for ministry. While over the years most congregations in the U.S. have been driven by nurture (focusing on the needs of those already in the church), they will now have to rediscover a passion for mission. Churches can no longer assume that people will be enculturated into the ministry from birth on. To be effective, congregations will now have to move from a focus on second-generation believers exclusively to first-generation converts. Such a focus will mean finding creative ways to reach those unconnected to the church. The traditional music and forms of the church, while important and meaningful for churched people, simply don't resonate with a "de-churched" culture. Reaching new generations requires new methods and new language. And that new language will certainly include some form of pop music.

Many mainstream congregations of different shapes, sizes, and locations have come to realize that churches can no longer do business as usual. That realization has led, at least in part, to the Contemporary Worship Movement. A growing number of congregations see culturally relevant worship as one of the ways in which the Spirit is reaching new generations with the gospel.

About the Book

This book seeks to offer practical help for those called to the task of reaching new people through new styles of worship. The insights offered in these pages have been written by contemporary worship practitioners—people who have turned to culturally relevant worship in order to reach the nonchurchgoing people in their communities.

The book is divided into four parts:

■ **Part 1** offers an overview of contemporary worship along with theological, historical, and sociological reasons for its use in the church today.

■ **Part 2** provides practical insights into how to blend the best of traditional worship with the best of contemporary worship for a Spirited-Traditional Service. The resource kit at the end of the section provides two sample services, two sample sermons, and an introductory listing of Spirited-Traditional choral songs.

■ **Part 3** looks at Contemporary Praise Services—participation-oriented services that use the heart language of new generations. The resource kit at the end of this section also includes some sample services and sermons along with several suggested worship choruses.

■ **Part 4** focuses on Seeker-Driven Services—contemporary worship services written for nonchurch-going people. Some will say that seeker services cannot in reality be called "worship" since only believers can and will worship God. As will be seen in this section, these services do lean toward outreach rather than pure worship. In fact, some "seeker" congregations, such as Willow Creek Community Church, don't refer to their Sunday services as worship. For them, worship takes place Wednesday and Thursday nights when the believers get together. Sunday is outreach and inspiration time. However, even nonchurched people, for the most part, understand that Sunday is a time when religious people worship or "do church." Seeker services build on that vague idea of "church" and try to make the service accessible for those who have never been there before. And since these services generally take place during traditional times of worship, seeker services are, for the purposes of this book, hung on the hook of worship. The resource kit at the end of part 4 includes, in addition to sample services and sermons, dozens of contemporary performance songs and three sample dramas.

While parts 2 to 4 deal with three specific kinds of contemporary worship, each section contains articles that will shed light on any form of worship. Although you may choose to implement only one of these suggested worship formats in your church, the entire book will serve to make that service the best it can be.

Thanks

Special thanks go to all the people who contributed to this book: Thanks for the great insights you've shared. We know that many congregations will discover a new passion for ministry and mission because of your willingness to share with others what you've been learning.

Thanks, too, to our PC. How did people ever write books before computers?

Finally, thanks to Jesus, who will build his church no matter how much the world changes. We're just glad he invites us along for the ride.

Tim and Jan Wright

Part 1

AN INTRODUCTION TO CONTEMPORARY WORSHIP

*We further believe, teach, and confess
that the community of God in every place
and at every time
has the right, authority, and power
to change, to reduce, or to increase ceremonies
according to its circumstances,
as long as it does so without frivolity and offense
but in an orderly and appropriate way,
as at any time may seem to be
most profitable, beneficial, and salutary
for good order, Christian discipline, evangelical
decorum,
and the edification of the church.*

—The Formula of Concord,
Solid Declaration, Article X,
paragraph 9

Worship in a Changing Culture

WILLIAM M. EASUM

Christian worship is undergoing a fundamental change for the first time. Throughout our history, in North America and other places influenced by the European Reformation, worship was based on three things: (1) the printed page, (2) a sixteenth-century appreciation of music, and (3) a culture that embraced Christianity. All three of these foundations are disappearing from North American culture, as they have also been disappearing from the post–World War II European cultures.

These changes are being driven by two phenomena. The first is television, especially MTV, which is exported all over the world. Its fast-paced, ever-changing, plugged-in-and-turned-up, visually oriented culture is making it harder than ever for the average young adult to experience the gospel in traditional church worship.

The second phenomenon is the rise of a generation of people who did not receive any spiritual or religious instruction from the home, school, or community. Many of these young adults have never been inside a church in their adult life, with the exception of baptisms, weddings, and funerals. Still, these young adults are on an intense spiritual journey. However, their journey is different from that of their parents. They want to celebrate the sacredness of life more than mourn their sinfulness. Their journey is spiritual, not necessarily religious, and is energized by cultural intrigue. When they do attend worship, they bring questions and expectations that are different from those who grew up in the church.

Because of these changes, traditional worship is becoming less and less meaningful to more and more people. Traditional styles of music and the linear, somber, slow forms of printed liturgy are no longer a fertile context for experiencing the gospel. Of all established Protestant churches, 80 to 85 percent are either plateaued or declining. Improvement in the quality of our present worship is not the

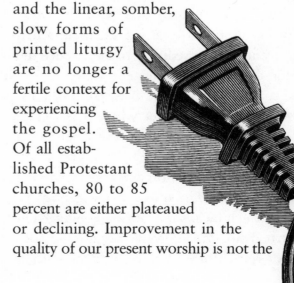

answer for most churches who have two constituencies, as Lyle Schaller put it: one in the nursing home and the other in the cemetery.

After a lengthy discussion on contemporary worship, a woman in her seventies approached me with this question: "Why can't these young people learn to like my music?" I responded: "Why can't you learn to like their music?" She thought for a moment and then made a remarkably insightful reply. "The answer is the same, isn't it?"

For the next twenty years, established churches need to provide a "two-track" system of worship. The "traditional track" is for those who like worship to include a hymnal, creeds, quiet time, and traditional church music. The "contemporary track" is for those who like worship to include a visual experience, not much quiet time, and indigenous music that is plugged-in and turned-up. The further we go into the twenty-first century, the less we should rely on track one and the more we should increase the visibility of track two.

The contemporary track is much more difficult to select because our musicians prefer traditional church music, our pastors grew up in the church, and many of our laity loathe contemporary music. However, when the contemporary track is provided with the same quality as the traditional track, unchurched young adults are more likely to experience the gospel and learn our language of faith.

The contemporary track of worship has distinctive elements no matter where it is found: (1) The service is more a time of celebration than a time of meditation. (2) Visual presentations of the gospel are more important than the printed page. (3) The music is indigenous to the area, which means it is normally plugged in and turned up. *Music* is the ritual—the soul music of the culture is more influential than inherited language. (4) Worship is understood to be a drama in which flow and the elimination of dead spots is essential. (5) The sermon is functional, with the language couched in phrases understood by secular people who are simultaneously skeptical and hurting inside.

An easy way to determine if your worship is on the contemporary track is by audiotaping the service and then playing it back with your eyes shut. Listen for two things: (1) Count the number of times no sound occurs for more than five seconds. If more than one or two such occurrences exist, the service is not contemporary. Dead spots are like losing the television picture while watching your favorite program. When they occur, people either panic or change the channel. (2) Ask yourself, "Which is the service most like, a basketball game, where people express their ecstasy and agony, or a funeral lament, where people express more pain and anguish than celebration?" If it is closer to a funeral lament, it is not contemporary worship.

Note that sometimes there is lamentation when making the change from a funerary service to a celebration of the good news. More pastors lose their pulpit and more laypeople are turned off by attempting to provide a contemporary alternative than any other form of new ministry. Proceed with caution, but proceed, for your lives depend on it.

The Rev. William M. Easum is a member of the Southwest Texas Annual Conference of The United Methodist Church. He currently serves as the senior consultant and executive director of 21st Century Strategies, Inc., a nonprofit organization devoted to retooling pastors, churches, and denominational leaders for ministry in a new world. He is the author of several books including, *How to Reach Baby Boomers, Dancing with Dinosaurs, The Complete Ministry Audit,* and *Sacred Cows Make Gourmet Burgers,* all published by Abingdon Press.

Making the Gospel Accessible Through Worship

TIM WRIGHT

The Word became a human being and lived here with us.
(JOHN 1:14 CEV)

Johnny was sitting in his playpen when Grandpa entered the room. As soon as he saw Grandpa, Johnny stood up, lifted his hands and said, "Out, Grandpa, out!" Grandpa was about to pick up his grandson when he heard Johnny's mom say, "Oh no you don't, Johnny! You're not getting out of that playpen! You're being punished!"

Grandpa watched as Johnny's eyes filled with big tears. It touched his heart. He wanted to pick up his grandson. But he didn't want to make Johnny's mom mad. So with no other options available to him, Grandpa climbed into the playpen with Johnny. He made himself accessible to his grandson by entering his world.

The heart of the gospel proclaims that God made himself accessible to us. Instead of demanding that we somehow find him, God came to us in the person of Jesus. Rather than expecting us to work through all the barriers that keep us from him (e.g., our sin, our finite understanding of God,

and so on), God climbed into our world. By becoming human, God took on the trappings of secular culture. He wore the clothes of the day. He spoke the language of the people. He ate their food. He visited their homes. He spent time with secular people like prostitutes, beggars, and tax collectors. He even partied with some of them. He attended a wedding and turned water into wine. In other words, God completely immersed himself in the culture and the human predicament that he wanted to change—without compromising himself or his message. He made himself accessible by becoming like the people he wanted to reach.

Making the Gospel Accessible

The history of Christianity has followed that same pattern. By taking the lead from the example of Jesus, believers throughout the centuries have tried to make the gospel as accessible and understandable as possible.
• Instead of using long, unintelligible theological discussions like the other religious

leaders of the day, Jesus told simple stories. He used illustrations from everyday life and poured God's truth into them.

● On Pentecost the disciples, empowered by the Spirit, spoke in tongues—in the languages of the people in the crowd. As a result, God made the gospel accessible to many different cultures.

● The apostle Paul, while preaching in Athens, pointed to a readily identifiable cultural, religious item (Acts 17:16-34). He drew the attention of his audience to one of their statues, which was dedicated to the unknown God. Paul praised their interest in religious matters and then told them how they could know this unknown God. In other words, Paul started with their culture in order to lead them to the truth of the gospel. Paul was committed to being all things to all people, to being accessible to all people, that he might reach some (1 Cor. 9:19-23).

● The authors of the New Testament wrote in Koine Greek—the common language of the people. Rather than using the language of the upper class and the educated, the writers of the Bible opted to use the vernacular that common people could understand. These authors chose to make the gospel accessible.

● During an Arts and Entertainment presentation called, "Who Wrote the Bible," a Jewish scholar, commenting on the Latin translation of the Hebrew Bible, said, "In translating the Bible from Hebrew into another language, the religious leaders were essentially saying, 'We don't care what language you speak. The message is important, and we want you to understand it.'"

● John Wycliffe attempted to make the gospel accessible to the people of his day by translating the Bible from Latin into English. He was branded a heretic and actually lost his life because of it. (And you thought it was tough trying to add a contemporary service to your worship menu!)

● The Reformation, at least in part, focused on making the gospel available to the people of God. During that time, if a person couldn't read or understand Latin, he or she was entirely dependent on the educated clergy to hear the gospel. And except for the stories told in the murals and stained glass that were represented in the popular art of the day, the gospel was inaccessible to ordinary people. One of Martin Luther's greatest accomplishments was to translate the Bible into common German so that his fellow Germans could understand it.

● Over two hundred years ago a young man leaned against a monument called the "market cross" in the industrial ghetto of Liverpool, England. He looked over the mass of dirty, grimy miners and millers. He listened as they spewed out their anger through cursing and drunken brawls. His heart ached to reach them for Christ. The young man took a deep breath and began to sing,

> O for a thousand tongues to sing
> My great Redeemer's praise,
> The glories of my God and King,
> The triumphs of His grace! [1]

He had written the words in honor of the first anniversary of his conversion to Christianity. The melody came from a popular tune that the people recognized. The familiar music, along with the joy-filled words captured the hearts of the people on the streets. Charles Wesley, using music from the culture, was able to connect with secular people and share the love of Christ with them.

● To make herself accessible, Mother Teresa identifies with the people she is trying to reach. She incarnates the gospel by living with them, eating with them, and caring for them.

● In seminary, I was trained to use the up-to-date tools available for counseling. We didn't think that using these "secular" or "modern" forms of therapy compromised the gospel. We saw these personality insights as vehicles for more effectively communicating the hope of the gospel with hurting people—for making the gospel available to people in crisis.

The gospel has always been about a God who makes himself accessible to secular people—a God who uses the stuff of culture to reach it and transform it.

Culturally Relevant Worship

The Contemporary Worship Movement is one more facet of God's work of reaching people. It uses the styles and language of secular people in order to communicate the truth of the gospel with them. To say it another way, contemporary worship seeks to make worship culturally relevant. Like the generations of believers before them, those using contemporary forms of worship want to translate the gospel in such a way that people today can understand it and be transformed by it.

Contemporary worship attempts to remove some of the religious barriers that keep people from church. For instance, secular people are unfamiliar with our religious language (e.g., abstract concepts such as redemption, justification, grace, absolution, and so on). They don't know about our religious traditions (the Kyrie, the use of robes and other religious garments, the creeds, and so on). They don't understand many of our hymns ("I raise my Ebenezer!" *Pardon me?* "There is a balm in Gilead." *A what in where?*). Although that language, those traditions, and our hymns provide stability and meaning for believers raised within the culture, they represent barriers to secular people—barriers that secular people must first overcome before they can understand the unmerited grace offered in the Savior. Usually, those barriers prove to be too formidable, and they give up.

We no longer expect people to learn Hebrew before they can read the Bible. We don't tell them they have to understand Greek before they can know God. We don't even ask them to try to figure out the gospel by reading the King James Version: "O ye Corinthians, our mouth is open unto you, our heart is enlarged. Ye are not straitened in us, but ye are straitened in your own bowels. Now for a recompense in the same (I speak as unto my children), be ye also enlarged" (2 Cor. 6:11-13). *Huh? Enlarged bowels?* Instead, we remove those barriers by making the Bible understandable and accessible by translating it into common English usage. We do the same with works written by the great leaders of Christianity. For example, we don't insist that non-German-speaking people have to understand German before they can enjoy the teachings of Martin Luther. Rather, we translate his works into the language of the people.

Contemporary worship simply strives to do the same thing—to make the gospel accessible to a lost, broken, and hurting world. European music and forms of worship from the sixteenth to eighteenth centuries have great value for those raised with it. Such successful music persisted for four hundred years. But secular people, steeped in American pop culture and music, find sixteenth- to eighteenth-century European music and styles irrelevant, out of date, and unintelligible.

God is using the contemporary worship movement to capture the hearts of secular people all across North America and even the world. The question is, Can believers use the stuff of culture without compromising the message? Is it even appropriate? For the answer, look to Jesus: "We are people of flesh and blood. That is why Jesus became one of us" (Heb. 2:14 CEV).

NOTE

1. Charles Wesley, "O For a Thousand Tongues to Sing."

Defining Contemporary Worship

TIM WRIGHT

Contemporary worship has captured the imaginations of pastors and laypeople alike. And yet, what may be contemporary for some could well be traditional for others.

The word *contemporary* can be defined: "Marked by characteristics of the present period." Building on that we can define contemporary worship as "worship marked by characteristics of the present period." Where traditional, liturgical forms of worship value stability, uniformity, and identification with the past, contemporary worship thrives on innovation and a focus on the present.

Daniel T. Benedict and Craig Kennet Miller, in their book, *Contemporary Worship for the 21st Century,* observe that contemporary worship

> refers to a movement and a style of worship that focuses on the culturally accessible and relevant, on the new and innovative, on use of recent technologies of communication for the purpose of outreach to seekers and those who are disenchanted with more traditional styles of worship.[1]

Contemporary worship seeks to communicate the gospel in current, up-to-date language. Instead of using "Christianese," the language of the Christian culture, contemporary worship uses words and phrases well known to the society of the day. Rather than selecting music from centuries past, contemporary worship presents the gospel by using the styles of music that resonate with popular culture. Even the sermons take on a contemporary feel by focusing on the issues with which the present generation is dealing. In other words, contemporary worship sounds like and looks like, in many ways, contemporary culture. It uses the styles, symbols, and language familiar to a particular group of people, within a particular historical context, in order to communicate the gospel to them intelligibly.

By its nature, contemporary worship does and should change. For example, as the styles of music change, so should the styles of music used in worship. To continue using 1960s folk music for thirty to forty years, ultimately makes the folk service traditional.

Contemporary worship demands continuous re-evaluation and stylistic updating. At the same time it must be said that contemporary worship is neither faddish nor trendy. At its heart contemporary worship is the attempt to relate to God and praise God in the language of the people. As that language changes, so does the style, but not the substance and center of worship.

Contemporary Worship and Outreach

Congregations often consider offering a contemporary service because they want to use it as a tool for reaching secular, unchurched, contemporary people. But in so doing, many mistakenly assume that by simply adding contemporary music the service will automatically appeal to secular people. Using contemporary music, however, does not necessarily make the service "outreach-oriented." The music can be as current as the latest pop hit, but because the service might be written for and geared to churched people it may still create barriers to reaching new people. For example, the music, though stylistically contemporary, may use religious language that confuses the

unchurched. The leader of the worship choruses might assume that people know how to "do church." The message may deal with issues that relate only to the concerns of the churched. The climate for newcomers might seem cold or lukewarm at best. Perhaps the members talk exclusively with their friends. Many contemporary worship services, though initially developed for outreach purposes, target believers and reach only believers. Charismatic services, for instance, though musically contemporary, tend to be highly believer-oriented in that the needs of Christians set the agenda for the service. Most secular, nonchurched people would feel lost in such a setting. Developing contemporary services for believers is fine, as long as we admit that that's what we're doing.

What makes a contemporary service outreach-oriented is the target audience. An outreach-oriented contemporary service gears the entire service to the needs of unchurched people. It takes seriously the reasons why people stay away from church, and then tries to overcome those reasons. As a result, the service will downplay much of congregational participation because unchurched people don't know our religious "stuff." A contemporary outreach-oriented service will focus instead on presenting the gospel through special music (bands, solos, and so on), dramas, interviews, and the message. An outreach-oriented service will find creative ways to welcome guests without making them feel embarrassed. It will use messages written for people who have never really heard the gospel before—messages that may come across as somewhat simplistic to those raised in the faith. A contemporary worship service is only outreach-oriented when the primary target, secular people, sets the agenda.

Defining Terms

To further understand contemporary worship it may help to identify some common terms often associated with the movement:

Seekers, the Unchurched, Secular People: While each has a unique shade of meaning, all three refer to people currently unconnected to a church or to a relationship with Christ. Their lives and values are not shaped by the values of the gospel. Seekers, specifically, are actively searching for the answers to their spiritual questions.

Believer-Oriented Worship: Worship geared exclusively to the needs, values, and priorities of those already committed to Christ and the church. This would include all traditional, liturgical, denominational worship services. It also includes contemporary services written for believers. In these services it is assumed, consciously or subconsciously, that there will be no visitors or seekers.

Believer-Oriented, Seeker-Friendly Worship: While the worship and messages focus on believers, great care is taken to help visitors feel welcome. Perhaps the service is printed out in its entirety in the bulletin, making it easy to follow. Maybe a team of greeters is trained to welcome people at the door of the sanctuary. Perhaps extra care is taken in choosing hymns that are easier to sing. Both traditional and contemporary believer services can be made seeker-friendly, though it admittedly takes a great deal of work to do so with traditional, liturgical forms of worship. This service assumes that visitors may be present, though the overwhelming majority of worshipers will be believers.

Seeker-Oriented Worship: A service geared specifically to the needs of those not currently enculturated by the church or the gospel. As much as possible, religious barriers are removed—that is, religious terms are recast into contemporary language; contemporary music, rather than organ music, is used; the messages deal with everyday life from a gospel perspective. This service assumes that seekers will be in the audience, and that believers might also attend.

Participative Worship: Worship that actively involves the congregation through the singing of hymns or worship choruses and the reciting of creeds and prayers. Oftentimes newcomers can feel excluded because they don't know the songs or the creeds.

Presentational Worship: A service in which most of the "action" takes place on the stage. With the exception of a worship chorus or two, the audience actively participates very little. Instead, the up-front music, dramas, interviews, and messages present the gospel to newcomers in relevant, nonthreatening ways. Because these services often connect with the needs of newcomers, however, newcomers find themselves drawn into the service and participate through their applause, laughter, tears, thinking, and response to the message. (For more on these styles of worship, see *A Community of Joy: How to Create Contemporary Worship* by Tim Wright.[2])

The Roots of Contemporary Worship

While contemporary worship is a relatively new phenomenon in Christianity, it traces its roots back to the New Testament. Contemporary worship is the attempt to take Jesus' great commission seriously—to go into all the world making disciples of all peoples. And to carry that out, many congregations are turning to contemporary worship to make the gospel culturally relevant and accessible to new generations of people.

NOTES

1. Daniel T. Benedict and Craig Kennet Miller, *Contemporary Worship for the 21st Century: Worship or Evangelism* (Nashville: Discipleship Resources, 1994), 120.
2. Tim Wright, *A Community of Joy: How to Create Contemporary Worship* (Nashville: Abingdon Press, 1994).

Worship Expectations

Churched People *(Those raised in the church)*	**Unchurched Guests** *(Those without a church background)*
Worship God	Self-help
Participate in worship	Observe the service
Sermons oriented to Bible study	Need-oriented message
Fellowship/Recognition	Anonymity
Traditions	Contemporary expressions
"How can I serve?"	"What's in it for me?"
Familiar religious jargon	Language they can understand
Give	Get
Moving worship	A moving experience
We all worship alike	Innovation/Choices
Commitment	No pressure
Awe	Intimacy
Contemplation, periods of silence	Background music
Prelude music	Conversation
Formal	Informal
God language	Jesus language
"How can I grow in my faith?"	"How can I make my life work?"

Historic Truths in Contemporary Packaging

TIM WRIGHT

Contemporary worship, like other kinds of innovation in church life, has attracted its critics. Some people believe that in offering contemporary worship churches abandon the very essence of Christianity. So when a congregation chooses to offer an alternative service, others in the denomination may accuse them of having left the fold, or of "selling out" to the culture of success and unlimited growth.

When the arguments against contemporary worship are examined, much of the controversy centers on the difference between substance and style. Many critics of contemporary worship see no difference between form and content; for example, to be Lutheran is to use *The Lutheran Book of Worship*. Contemporary worship advocates, on the other hand, believe that style and substance are different, though related.

Substance: The real or essential part or element of anything; essence, reality, or basic matter. *(New World Dictionary)*

For purposes of discussion, substance, when used in a worship context, refers to the underlying theology of the denomination or congregation. Substance has to do with what we believe. For example, the substance of Lutheran worship includes the Lutheran understanding of the Word and Sacraments. For Pentecostals the substance of worship includes their theological understanding of the Baptism of the Holy Spirit. In other words, substance refers to the essence of our understanding of the gospel. The substance of faith and worship never changes.

Style: The manner or mode of expression in language, as distinct from the ideas expressed; way of using words to express thoughts. *(New World Dictionary)*

Style refers to the method or form used to communicate the substance. The style might be liturgical or contemporary, but the same substance is communicated through both. Where the substance never changes, styles do and must change. For the style expresses the substance. If the style is ineffective in communicating the substance—if it doesn't connect with the audience—then the style must be adjusted for a more effective presentation. We can have the most moving liturgy in the world, but if it doesn't relevantly communicate the substance of the gospel with a lost world, then the style must be redesigned or a new style must be created.

When I was lecturing in France about contemporary worship, I had to use an interpreter. My style of communication, English, wasn't connecting with those who spoke only French. Though the style changed (from English to French) the substance or essence of the lecture remained the same. The same is true in worship.

Worship is Lutheran, not because of the style used, but because of the theology expressed. A contemporary service is United Methodist when it shares the essence of the Wesleyan understanding of the gospel. Styles communicate the substance. Styles change, but the substance is eternal.

The Substance of Contemporary Worship

Contemporary worship, however, is not primarily about style. It is not driven by gimmicks or fads. Contemporary worship, like traditional worship, is driven by the message—the gospel of Jesus Christ. If the heart of the service is not rooted in the gospel, then contemporary worship will simply be a show. (The same can be said of Anglo-Catholic liturgical worship, with its color, texture, and smells.) But if contemporary elements are seen as a means to sharing the gospel, then contemporary worship will be a dynamic, powerful vehicle for reaching people. Effective contemporary services move people, not with drums, pop music, and drama, but with the message of Jesus relevantly communicated. The drums, pop music, and drama simply serve as tools for sharing the message.

Because contemporary worship often seeks to connect with the unchurched, certain themes can be seen in such services across denominational lines:

1. God loves you. Contemporary services want guests to know that Jesus is on our side; that God values us and believes in us; that God is for us.

2. God is accessible to you. Contemporary worship uses the culture of the day to let people know that God is not out of touch. God comes to us where we are, in our language and circumstances to offer us life. God is made known to us in Jesus.

3. God forgives you. People come to church broken and hurting, looking for healing and hope. Contemporary services share the good news that in Jesus Christ God forgives us unconditionally—that in Jesus God can make us whole.

4. God can make a difference in your life. Contemporary services invite people to discover the difference Jesus can make in our daily lives. By focusing on issues that people deal with every day, contemporary services remind us that God cares about all aspects of our lives. God promises to walk through all of life with us, supporting us, encouraging us, empowering us, and getting us through.

5. God wants to be your friend. People today value intimacy in their relationship with God. Contemporary worship services by nature are more intimate and relational than traditional services. The very atmosphere of the service reinforces the relational aspect of Christianity. Contemporary services let people know that they can be friends with their Creator through Jesus. He is a Savior and friend who will never let us down.

Again, the essence of effective contemporary services is found in a biblically based, gospel-centered, historically rooted message. The style of worship simply seeks to communicate that message as effectively and relevantly as possible.

Contemporary Worship Through the Lens of Traditional Worship

ANDY LANGFORD

Don't throw out the baby with the bath water! Traditional worship still has much to offer contemporary worship. In the rush toward creative, experimental, user-friendly, contemporary worship, worship leaders must be careful not to cast off the past for the sake of the present. In our desire to develop new liturgical forms, learn new music, and preach in new ways, pastors, musicians, and others who plan and lead worship must remember and often incorporate the liturgical contributions of the saints who have sustained the church for two millennia.

The historic forms of worship are today expressed in the hymnals and books of worship of the old mainline churches (Episcopal, Lutheran, Presbyterian, United Church of Christ, United Methodist). These hymnals and books of worship are serious and thoughtful attempts to express the Christian faith in ways faithful to both the present day and to the traditions of the church universal. In the movement toward contemporary worship, however, there is a tendency to throw out these hymnals and books of worship, replacing them with overhead projections of trendy choruses. Bulletins are no longer used. As a seeker of valid forms of contemporary worship, do not forget the resources that have brought us this far.

Based on patterns of worship from the earliest church, the mainline hymnals and books of worship have nurtured and still minister to millions of persons. All these hymnals and books of worship reveal several fundamental touchstones that all who call themselves Christian should hold in common, and that must be retained in any service of worship. In the midst of the massive change now sweeping worship forms, it is too easy to overlook these foundation stones of worship. To overlook them however, rejects not only our rich liturgical heritage, but also submits us to the tyranny of the personal and the transient.

The style, language, instruments, media, music, and other aspects of worship may change, but there are four essential elements of worship that are neglected at great peril to the Body of Christ: (1) the Word of God read aloud, proclaimed, and heard; (2) the sacraments of Baptism and Holy Communion rightly taught and practiced; (3) prayer offered and received; and (4) fellowship in the community by word and sign. Effective congregational worship, either traditional or contemporary, must emphasize regularly and consistently, all four of these essential elements.

The Word of God

The Word of God read, proclaimed, and heard is the cornerstone of every service of worship. If there is no Word of and from God, there is no worship. Each service of the traditional hymnals and service books is designed from the Word of God. The tendency of many contemporary services is to focus on contemporary issues facing individuals and the community, and as an event, this style is inconsistently focused on human concerns instead of our need and obligation to worship the Lord. If your services start in this way, remember that it is the Word of God alone that provides the answers.

The Bible as a sacred document should be visible, seen, and used in Christian worship, not as an icon or idol, but as the source of the revelation of God's Word for us. By flashing biblical passages on a projector screen, we treat the Word as temporary E-mail. Hold in one's hand a Bible, touch it, and read aloud the Word of God.

The richness and fullness of the Scripture can be opened to the people, even those who come with no literary appreciation of it. Don't throw out the lectionary too quickly.

Lectionaries were created, beginning in the fourth century C.E. as a tool for oral persons so that they might hear the good news. If we notice that the culture is becoming more visual and oral, rather than print oriented, remember that this is not the first time. Images, icons, and art, along with reading the lections of scripture aloud, sustained the people of God through more than three quarters of the Christian era. Too many contemporary services use only a small fraction of the scripture, predominantly using one-sentence texts from the Gospels and Epistles. Too few narratives are read, and rarely is an entire book taught. Contemporary preachers tend to create their own canon within the canon—apart from the discernment of a wider Christian consensus, and thus forget the height, and depth, and breadth of the scriptures. It is remarkable how often the text of the day will deal with contemporary issues that you might not have considered. While you may not wish to use all three lessons and the psalm from the lectionary, using one text a week will keep the message on a biblical foundation.

Simply reading scripture, however, is by itself not sufficient for faithful worship. Preaching the Word links the scripture with human life. Protestant worship is incomplete without a sermon, however delivered, outlined, or related to the music and drama of the day. While technical feats might awe a boomer audience, avoid tendencies to let a drama or video clips *substitute* for the Word proclaimed. The rise of narrative preaching, and didactic preaching (both of which are typical in contemporary worship), can be faithful to the text and engaging of contemporary audiences. Good preaching still demands personal devotion, serious study, adequate preparation, and major attention to a particular community of faith.

Reading and preaching the Word, however, are still not enough. To become flesh, the Word of God must call forth a response from those who hear. Persons in the congregation must be able to answer the question at the end of the service, "So what?" It is a major contribution of contemporary worship that reading and preaching the Word must relate to the listeners. The best of contemporary worship ensures that the preaching includes time, space, and opportunities for persons to say yes. Prayers, testimonies, hymns, offerings, and a multitude of other responses enable individuals and congregations to answer the call of God. Resist the temptation to let the preaching be a presentation alone, a "thought for the day," but instead preach to offer persons the grace of God.

The Sacraments

Baptism and the Lord's Supper comprise the second foundation stone of worship. Baptism calls persons into Christian discipleship, and the Lord's Supper offers food for the journey. Some contemporary worship minimizes these essential rites of grace by reducing the texts into sound bites, speeding up the actions, and minimizing their significance, lest they become a scandal to the uninitiated. These sign acts of divine intervention can still be powerful moments of contemporary worship.

Baptism provides individuals and congregations the opportunity to take a stand against the forces of evil in contemporary culture, profess Jesus Christ as Lord and Savior, and commit themselves to Christian service. The best of contemporary worship emphasizes this turning from evil toward Christ with services that include water, singing, and testimonies. There is no more powerful visual and aural rite than the washing of a new believer by water and the Spirit. Contemporary worship itself stands as a testimony that in each new generation Christians are made, not born. Baptism is the certain sign of one's incorporation into the Body of Christ. If such signs of God's grace are privatized and withdrawn from seeker services, the worship event is not following the example of Jesus, and seekers are denied a clear perception of the cost of discipleship in a very dangerous world.

The Lord's Supper is clearly an invitation to be in community with others in worship and with our Savior. In all the church hymnals and books of worship, the Eucharist is the primary response by the community to the Word of God read and proclaimed; and so it should remain. Because the holy meal involves action, fellowship, and food, it fits well into contemporary patterns of worship and can easily be celebrated even more frequently. Increasingly, congregations celebrate the meal weekly, and we still have much to learn from African American congregations who celebrate the meal with fervor.

Prayer

Prayer is the primary means through which all worshipers communicate with God, and is the third foundation stone of both traditional and contemporary worship. Formal and free prayer are both appropriate in the community gathered to honor the Lord. The historic prayers of the church as well as those composed by the sensitive souls of our time are important means through which the church speaks and listens to God. Prayers may be spoken or silent, led by laity or clergy, printed or prayed extemporaneously. The historic church, by its variety, prevents the people at worship from falling into self-centered ruts or narcissistic pleas for self and family alone. And do not forget the Psalms, the prayers and laments of the Bible. These heartfelt conversations with God often speak of contemporary needs.

Fellowship

Christians grow in grace and faith when they gather with one another. While contemporary worship tends toward presentation, with an emphasis on the congregation as audience, worship should exhibit a congregation's love and deepen their relationships with one another. Although we need to focus on primary audiences, our worship most pleases God when it is open to people of all ages, conditions, races, and backgrounds. Don't exclude anyone from worship. Use the gifts of the community gathered for prayer and sharing of gifts and experiences. Worship must not be pastor/leader centered but people centered. Use the talents of artists, dancers, musicians, and dramatists in your community often.

Music is the most effective way to bind a community together in fellowship. Through song, congregations share their faith and experience community. Resist the temptation to always perform contemporary music, and use the vast range of music and hymnody from throughout the ages. Don't assume too quickly that any one audience cares only about one style of music. Don't assume that a soul music for a particular generation (such as boomers or

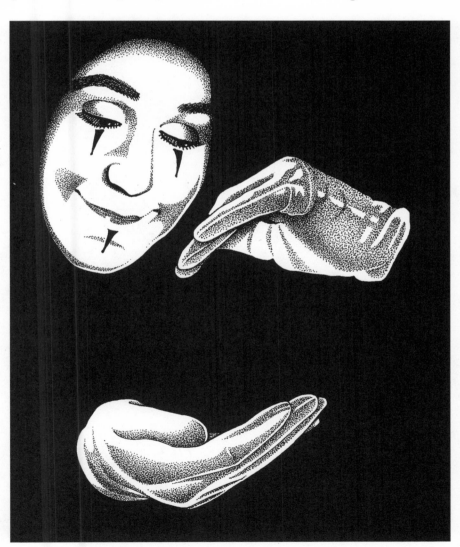

busters) remains "contemporary" if that is the only music that is played as the generation ages. Too much of any one thing leads to the sour observation that there is "nothing new under the sun."

Experiment. Break new ground. Try new patterns of worship. But as you do, do not forget the four foundation stones of worship. Ministry through the Word, the sacraments, prayer, and fellowship enables God to call people to discipleship and enables the community gathered to respond to that call. By emphasizing these four foundations in con-

temporary worship, the Body of Christ will continue to proclaim God's good news in each new age.

Andy Langford was the general editor of *The United Methodist Book of Worship* and chair of the international, ecumenical committee that created the Revised Common Lectionary. He also edited the new *Cokesbury Chorus Book 1*. His book, *Blueprints for Worship* (Abingdon Press), shows how to use the traditional rites of the church in contemporary settings. Andy now serves as copastor of First United Methodist Church in China Grove, North Carolina, where he incorporates acts of contemporary worship into traditional liturgical forms.

Contemporary Worship and the Reformation

DAVID S. LUECKE

What can we learn about approaches to worship from the sixteenth-century Reformation that gave birth to Protestantism? What kind of worship would Martin Luther himself choose to lead today? We could choose nearly any of the Reformers to explore this matter, but Luther generates the most heat when questions of relevance are raised.

The answer to the above question depends on whether you look at Luther's writings or at Luther's cultural context. The first approach is concerned with his writing of the Latin Mass (1523) and his translation of it into the German Mass (1526). Such a study of the text concludes that Luther obviously preferred the classic liturgical form he had inherited, with its distinct components that build toward celebrating the Lord's Supper each Sunday.

In this country, the liturgical renewal movement that flourished in the 1950s to the 1970s, and was fueled by Vatican II dialogue, is encouraged by this kind of textual approach to worship. This can be called, "The Restoration Story" of worship, which says: "Luther recognized the classic liturgy as best. So should we. Let's update our worship by restoring those old textual forms." This is by far the dominant understanding of worship practices in Lutheran circles today. And the same liturgical renewal movement has touched most major Protestant denominations after Vatican II.

Another, and better, way to think about this search for origins is to say: "Let's look more closely at what was going on in those formative years of the 1520s. The principles that drove Luther's choices are what will prove to be most instructive for the leader in our time." This kind of reasoning, whether through appeal to Luther, Wesley, or other founders of large movements, is very appealing to those who develop alternative or contemporary worship forms—because the reformers themselves were taking huge risks against the establishment of their time.

Even the most recent editor in English of Luther's works on liturgy thinks that

> This whole idea of restoring the sunken glory of ancient ritual is a product of nineteenth century Romanticism and was as foreign to Luther as to the Romanist theologians of his day. . . . Luther would have been nonplused by the plaudits (for retaining the Mass), as though the preservation of ancient forms was a liturgical mark of merit.[1]

Concern for the Weak in Faith

The crucial reasoning or principle that guided the development of worship in the Reformation was "concern for the spiritual well-being of the weak in faith." The choice of worship forms is not a matter of personal preference but must depend on the need of the followers.[2] Luther's motivation was a strong love for people weak in faith, who were already experiencing cultural chaos during the Reformation. The people needed no more change than necessary in their conflict with Roman officials.

Worship is external to the spiritual recognition and living out of justification by grace through faith, which was the driving principle behind the reforms that were developed.

As externalities, the forms of worship were really not important to the spiritual matters of consequence. Since there is no harm in traditional liturgical forms used properly, the principle was to use what the people knew. Liturgical scholar James F. White explains that the historical ceremonies and rites "were firmly lodged in popular piety, and Luther saw no need to trample on them."[3] Luther wanted to reshape an existing Christian piety, not destroy it, as he feared would happen with too many changes in the externalities of worship.

Reformation historian E. G. Schwiebert, in *Luther and His Times: The Reformation from a New Perspective*, documents how

> The Deutsche Messe (German Mass) was regarded by Luther as a kind of colorful Sunday dress for those not yet strong enough in the faith. In time he hoped to dispense with the outward glitter and display of vestments, incense, candles, etc. and to provide more mature congregations with simple preaching, prayers and hymn singing; but unfortunately he did not yet have a congregation ready for removal of such props.[4]

A love for the weak in faith also motivates the developers of contemporary worship in the present day. We long for those times when all are believers and we can gather with simple heartfelt prayer, hymns, and preaching. But we also want to help those seekers with weak faith, who are not drafted by parents, or forced by authorities in the state, to come to our meeting places.

A Question of Unity

The Restoration approach to liturgy seeks uniformity in worship practices among congregations and denominations. The liturgy is praised with adjectives such as *universal* and *fundamental* over time and across cultures. Because Jesus prayed that we would all be in unity (John 17), meaning that we would not hate one another as the world does, a universal form of worship is proposed as a good basis for expanding Christian unity among congregations and church bodies.

But uniformity in worship forms was not an objective for the Reformers, is not part of Jesus' prayer in the Gospel of John, and was not even desirable in principle. The Restoration story about worship proposes that Luther had to be forced to present a simplified Mass in German because he feared that it would detract from the real, full Latin Mass. Another way of receiving the story is that Luther indeed felt forced and reluctant to present a simplified Mass, not because he feared it would detract from the Latin Mass, but because he feared that anything he presented would be taken as an ideal pattern for every congregation to follow. As with his Latin Mass entitled "For the Church at Wittenberg," what he drew up this time was meant for Wittenberg.

This reformer thought it most important to design worship with due regard for local customs and needs. Vajta demonstrates that Luther was also skeptical about working out a church constitution in detail for fear other churches would adopt it and thus disregard existing customs within the congregation. This kind of imitation would fail to adapt to the given situation, perhaps even succumbing to legalism.[5]

Luther feared widespread uniformity. He saw two dangers. One was legalism, which strikes at the heart of the Reformation. The other was failure to adapt to the needs of those being served. Thus an absolute liturgi-

cal fixation was wrong in principle. "Outward things should remain free, and the truth that the unity of the church consists in one faith in the one gospel, not in the uniformity of outward forms in worship, should not be obscured."[6]

To keep people from assigning too much importance to the form of the service, Luther claimed that love for others will call for many changes, even as a tree sprouts new blooms and fruit every year. But changes should be made in an orderly manner. Luther's principle of love and regard for common people made him the sworn enemy of arbitrary changes.

Whether you defend the restoration of some "classic" pattern for worship of the Lord, or whether you defend the freedom to make changes in "external" things, you can take a lesson from history, which is a relentless reminder of diversity. The Reformation spread to many different towns and independent districts, among many tribes and ethnicities. Each developed its own church order for organization and regulation, including directions for worship. By 1555 there were 135 church orders, and more in the Scandinavian countries. By 1580 the last of the unifying Reformation confessions, the Formula of Concord, established the principle that "the community of God in every place and at every time has the right, authority, and power to change, to reduce or to increase ceremonies according to its own circumstances."[7]

Implications

What can we conclude for worship practices today based on this quick overview of the Reformer's approach?

1. Don't let one set of worship practices become a basis for establishing unity in a church body. A denomination may then gradually lose effectiveness in the diversity of circumstances where it is called to minister. An even more important concern is to avoid liturgical legalism, which is counter to the Reformation purpose of giving ordinary people access to the good news in Jesus Christ.

2. All worship should demonstrate a love for the weak in faith. Oftentimes highly developed classic liturgical forms are presented as mature worship for spiritually fit believers. Maturity, which is easily confused with elitism, is precisely the wrong reason for advocating the use of classical forms in a congregation. Mature Christians ought to be able to worship within any Christ-centered format. Pick worship practices that are most supportive of the immature.

3. Be careful about abruptly changing worship forms and practices in an established congregation. (Be advised that the best plan is to introduce new worship forms in a new service or a new congregation.) Respect those whose weakness may well be dependence on traditional or classical liturgical worship. Again, the externalities of worship forms are not the most basic part of the Christian life anyway.

4. Don't let the weakness of traditionalists blind a congregation to the weakness of others whom the church leaders are called to reach. The unchurched are by definition weak in Christian faith. Their need for easier access to the dynamics of worship logically can lead to different worship practices. Again, don't let the externalities of worship stand in the way of the mission-driven leaders.

5. Established congregations can serve different sets of weakness by offering two or more different styles of worship.

When pursued with integrity, which means a thorough and Christ-centered focus and sensitivity, contemporary forms of worship fit well with the spirit and purpose of the Reformation. Indeed, these practices fit well with the new reformation that has already begun on the Protestant landscape.

NOTES

1. Ulrich S. Leupold, ed. *Luther's Works, Volume 53: Liturgy and Hymns* (Minneapolis: Fortress Press, 1965), xiv.

2. Vilmos Vajta, *Luther on Worship* (Philadelphia: Muhlenberg Press, 1959), 84, 86.

3. James F. White, *Protestant Worship: Traditions in Transition* (Louisville: Westminster/John Knox Press, 1989), 43.

4. E. G. Schwiebert, *Luther and His Times: The Reformation from a New Perspective* (St. Louis: Concordia, 1950), 668.

5. Vajta, *Luther on Worship*, 182.

6. Franz Lau, *Luther's Works*, trans. Robert H. Fischer (Louisville: Westminster, 1953), 98.

7. Vajta, *Luther on Worship*, 177, 183.

David S. Luecke is the founding pastor of Community of Hope Church in Brecksville, Ohio, and administrative pastor of Royal Redeemer Lutheran Church in North Royalton, Ohio. He is the author of *Evangelical Style and Lutheran Substance, New Designs for Church Leadership* (both published by Concordia), and *The Other Story of Lutherans at Worship: Reclaiming Our Heritage of Diversity* (The Fellowship Ministries).

Contemporary Worship in a Rural Setting

JEFFREY H. PATTON

Jesus said, "Yet a time is coming and has now come when the true worshipers will worship the Father in spirit and truth, for they are the kind of worshipers the Father seeks" (John 4:23 NIV). The evolution and development of numerous worship formats throughout the history of the Christian church has been and continues to be a witness to the church's ongoing struggle to fulfill these words of Jesus. Today, the church continues to experiment with the forms of worship without changing the substance of the worship experience. Contemporary formats that have emerged in recent years and those now emerging are continuations of this process.

Some traditional worship leaders assert that contemporary formats will not work in a rural setting. I have heard a few people say that such worship changes shouldn't even be attempted in rural areas. Others tell me that their parishioners won't stand for it. On the other hand, many pastors and many more parishioners tell me of the frustration of sitting through worship experiences that no longer speak to their hearts or minds. For many people in rural settings (especially those people fifty years of age and younger), traditional worship formats are no competition for catching up on the farm work, watching TV, or napping. Whether we like it or not, the medium and the methods of conveying the message of the gospel must change if we are to realize the goal of reaching the hearts and souls of the post–World War II generations. To those who insist that it cannot be done in the rural setting, come and see.

At the East Canton United Methodist Church (126 members) the worship format is contemporary. The service is relaxed, laughter is frequent, noise is abundant, music is the medium, and Christ is the center. The pastor never wears a robe and is rarely in a tie. Numerous people have varied roles each week and help conduct the service. Choruses and hymns are intermixed and accompanied by piano, guitars, flutes, and other instruments.

The East Canton Church is located in north central Pennsylvania approximately forty minutes south of Elmira, New York, and fifty minutes north of Williamsport, Pennsylvania. The region is dominated by agricultural interests and has recently seen an influx of senior citizens. The area consists of four thousand households within a ten-mile radius. The last census showed a decrease in the population and a further decrease is expected. The racial make-up of the community is 98.8 percent white. The average age is thirty-eight and the average household income is $27,544. Rural working families compose 42.2 percent of the population. Country seniors, aging retirees, and spirited seniors make up 9.2 percent of the community. Those aged twenty-five to fifty make up 46.9 percent of the population (Church Information and Development Services, 10/19/92).

Over the years it became clear to our leadership that we were not reaching those aged eighteen to fifty. As is true in similar parts of the nation, those in this age group were not interested in worship styles based on an eighteenth-century model. In 1986 the order of worship at East Canton followed very closely the instructions contained in *The Book of Hymns* 1964.

To make the worship service format reflect a more contemporary atmosphere, the worship committee began to "gradually" (a key word) experiment with choruses, short songs, praise music, and easy to learn songs written in contemporary keys. Initially the new songs were sung only on the second Sunday of the month. The welcome to such a change was mixed initially, but soon that service became the most attended and talked about service during the month. A few of the supportive seniors resisted the changes made to the second Sunday service, but most "tolerated" it, especially when they saw how many new people were attracted to this small country church.

Soon after we started a Saturday night service that was even more reflective of contemporary worship formats. This

service featured extended singing—usually choruses and praise songs. The service also included a time for prayer in small groups. An emphasis on the dynamic presence of the Holy Spirit and the power of Jesus Christ to change lives, touch hearts, and heal wounds and sicknesses permeated our time together.

At the end of six months we evaluated all the worship services and concluded that the Sunday morning service needed more life. The Saturday night service was not meeting our expectations, although it proved a wonderful learning tool. We dropped the Saturday night service but used its format during the service on the second Sunday of the month. The core group of those who attended Saturday night and a growing number of younger families attracted to the contemporary service on the second Sunday of the month, began pushing for more changes at every Sunday service. By 1990 we embarked on a total restructuring of the Sunday service. Each service began to take on more contemporary elements and the results were dramatic. Within one year we outgrew our space. A building project ensued and growth continues to manifest itself. The resultant changes are giving life to our worship and helping people grow in their faith and commitment to Jesus Christ.

Your congregation has listed 126 persons as members, your average attendance at worship in 1993 was 119. This is approximately a 97 percent attendance to membership ratio and has placed you in the highest percentile of our annual conference. This also places you ahead of 81.6 percent of all United Methodist Churches in the United States. (Report prepared by the Director of Parish Development of the Central Pennsylvania Conference, Thomas Irwin, Jr., 3/8/95.)

The high ratio of worship attendance to membership is usually very good evidence that guests are finding the worship relevant and meaningful.

The following schedule provides an example of our rural contemporary worship format. (The service officially begins at 9:30 A.M.).

9:20 A.M. Choruses and lively hymns

9:30 A.M. Brief announcements

9:35 A.M. Extended singing—hymns and choruses

9:50 A.M. Testimony time or a time for sharing joys

10:00 A.M. Prayer time—conversational prayers, congregational participation

10:10 A.M. Children's time—usually a few songs along with a story and prayer

10:15 A.M. Special music/skit

10:20 A.M. Offering taken as worship choruses are sung

10:30 A.M. Scripture lesson and morning message

10:45 A.M. A hymn or chorus of commitment

10:50 A.M. Dismissal

10:52 A.M. Closing song—reflective of the morning theme

Of the ninety minutes we are together, over forty-five minutes are spent in song, usually led by piano and guitar. The songs are joyous, celebrative, and worshipful. The pastor's part in the service is the ten- to fifteen-minute message. Other people lead the remainder of the service.

While some say that contemporary worship formats won't work in rural settings, our church demonstrates the opposite. Not only have we adopted a more contemporary format, but we have also incorporated desirable aspects that larger congregations might not be able to accomplish. For example, the idea of sitting with five or six people in a small group and baring your hearts in prayer might be problematic in a large congregation due to lack of familiarity from week to week. One purpose of contemporary worship is to reach those who don't know the language of our faith. Our smaller, rural size actually enhances that relational objective.

Contemporary worship, which uses the heart language of the people, is the language that this church is learning to speak. Our experience has shown us that contemporary worship formats can lead people into a deeper level of commitment to Christ by enabling their whole selves to be embraced by their worship experience.

Contemporary worship is not for every-one—it takes a big risk to make significant changes in an old church—but when done gradually, lovingly, and under the direction of the Holy Spirit, we have found that many people's lives are touched by God. The Sunday morning service has gone from a spectator sport in the rural setting, to participant owned and driven. We have moved from talk about God to a dynamic sense of God's presence with us. I believe we are learning to worship "in spirit and in truth."

Jeffrey H. Patton graduated from Lycoming College (BA), Princeton Theological Seminary in Virginia (Th.M.), Union Theological Seminary in Virginia (Th.M.), and finished the residency portion of a Ph.D. in Pastoral Theology at Princeton Theological Seminary. He has published an article entitled "Pilot Study on Clergy Divorce—Reluctance to Seek Counseling." Currently, he is the pastor of two rural churches in north central Pennsylvania. In addition, he is the administrative director/pastor counselor of the Northern Tier Counseling Center located in Mansfield, Pennsylvania. He and his wife, Sandra Frymire, have two children, Gregory and Michelle.

How to Add or Change a Service Without Splitting Your Church

BOB MOONEY AND CHERYL DRIVER

Pastor: "I want to torch the organ and bring in a rock band. The unchurched hate organ music!"

Director of Music: "O.K., but you know that we will both be out of a job after next Sunday!"

Following that conversation, Bob Mooney, pastor of Messiah Lutheran Church in Yorba Linda, California, and Cheryl Driver, Messiah's director of music, began the process of moving our very traditional liturgy toward a contemporary style of worship. What we do at Messiah won't work for every congregation. Through a variety of mistakes and outright failures, we have come to realize that no congregation can completely adopt the worship style of another. Even so, we have isolated some basic principles that are crucial to creating joyful worship—and increasing attendance.

Tradition: Our denominational practice requires us to strive continuously to have an orderly worship—worship that brings us face to face with our need for God's grace in meaningful, relevant messages, music, and prayer. Each worship service is to have integrity, flow, and consistency. That includes contemporary forms of worship. Effective contemporary worship services mean more than rock 'n' roll music, no vestments, and tennis shoes. Contemporary services, much like liturgical forms of worship, should help us connect with God's grace, which comes to us through Word and Sacrament. But the vexing question for church leaders is how to keep tradition *and* change the worship style or add a different style of worship. It can be done!

Patience: This is one of the most difficult attributes to learn and the most necessary in the long process of moving to or adding a contemporary service. And it will be a long process. After seven years Messiah now enjoys a liturgical order of service with the energy and joy of a contemporary sound. Instead of adding new worship services we chose to focus on improving our existing two services. We arrived at a blended uplifting service that incorporates traditional liturgy, praise songs, a band, *and* the organ! We eventually removed some parts of the liturgy through a process of adding and replacing. The basic liturgical structure, however, remains in place. Liturgical music has been replaced with praise songs, liturgical names have been changed (for example, the Kyrie to Prayer for Mercy), dead silences have been eliminated, and exciting, uplifting music has been added.

Vision: Envision the end result. Creating and promoting a strong vision helps in the process of making changes. Messiah is still working and will continue to work toward the vision that Bob had when he wanted to torch the organ. What we do today is the result of keeping our focus on the vision by setting small, reachable, intermediate goals. We "tweak" the service constantly. Most of the time it is not noticeable except to the worship leadership. But again, every change lines up with our vision for worship.

Music: Excellence is an adjective that should describe the

music used. The musicians must be excellent, dedicated, and committed to the type of music that you choose to use. In introducing new forms of music to the worship experience, the following tips may be helpful:

- Try to win the support of your existing musical leadership by holding up the vision behind the changes.
- Research your community's prevailing musical tastes—country, pop, alternative, and so on. What do people listen to on the radio?
- Introduce the new styles of music instrumentally at first. If your primary instrument has been the organ, begin to use the piano for offertories and preludes. Add other instruments with the piano by using the arrangements of songs you eventually want your congregation to know. When you add drums (and you will if you want the service to be contemporary)

make sure that your drummer is excellent and sensitive. Drums should add to the music, not be the focus. This is true for all your musicians. Your musical leadership should feel that they are not performing, but worshiping.

- Make your choir an asset. At Messiah, we still sing a few classical anthems. However, the choir has played a large part in "setting the stage" for our blended service by singing newer contemporary anthems 90 percent of the time. Many beautiful anthem arrangements of new praise music now exist.

- Introduce new music forms in small groups that include some type of worship in their meetings. Your congregation will become familiar with the songs and you will begin to gain subtle member support for your service changes. Five years ago during an annual couples retreat we began introducing and teaching new praise songs to the fifty-plus people who attended. Two wonderful things resulted. People asked if we could sing those songs in our worship service (we now had a request from the congregation to make some changes); and excellent musicians with a passion for contemporary music and worship came forward and volunteered their services.

Leadership: When changing or adding a worship service, consider the gifts of the pastor and the worship leaders. Having the right people for the right job is crucial if you want to make changes without splitting the church. If the pastor is not comfortable enough to listen to contemporary music, or is uncomfortable in the more informal set-

ting that contemporary worship demands, the service will have a hard time getting off the ground. The pastor and worship leaders need a contagious passion for new styles of worship. Offering a more traditional service with excellence will prove more effective in the long run than doing a contemporary service halfheartedly. It is best if your existing staff has the passion, gifts, and vision for creating a new worship service. Bringing in someone new, while at times necessary, takes time. It takes time for the new person to assimilate himself or herself to a new setting. It also takes time for the congregation to embrace and trust him or her, especially if the new person is to bring about some radical changes.

Awareness: Look at every part of your service with an "unchurched" eye. Is it confusing? Does the service assume that everyone knows the difference between page numbers and hymn numbers? (They don't!) Is it apparent when to stand or sit? Are the words "churchy"? The word *song* is more understandable than the word *hymn*. "Prayer for Mercy" will make more sense to people than "Kyrie." The word *greeting* will connect better than "passing the peace." By becoming aware of those who come with an unchurched background, you and your people will better appreciate why a new service is needed or why the current service needs some fine-tuning.

Resistance: You can effectively deal with resistance if you expect it, prepare for it, and LISTEN to it. Listening is an important part of what must happen in the change process. We need to listen to what is important to people, to what their "sacred cows" in worship might be, and to how they are responding to the changes. Many times listening can help prevent a conflict. In some situations at Messiah, in which people did not like a change, we simply listened to them and validated their feelings and concerns. As a result of this empathy, they became open to and accepting of the change. Through listening and openly responding to concerns, you can educate people as to why you added or changed the service. At Messiah, we have run into very little resistance because we have made the changes slowly, we have respected our tradition, we have striven for excellence, and we have focused on the strengths of the worship leaders. Our contemporary style has helped account for a dramatic 52 percent increase in worship attendance over the past four years (this kind of influx tends to diffuse resistance). Everything we do at Messiah, including worship, is held up to our mission statement—"To know Christ and to make Christ known." We intentionally tell our people that worship is an important part of evangelism. This intentionality allows members to understand why the church is embarking on this new journey. At Messiah we see more and more people bringing their friends and family to church. At least half of the new people now coming to worship come from a non-Lutheran background or from a completely unchurched background.

Prayer: Pray diligently for your worship services. Prayer is the power behind effective change, and it also makes known to you things that are gimmicks. Bear in mind that adding to what you are already doing is easier than starting from scratch. Always be sensitive to the makeup of the congregation, its history and traditions. Take it "slow and easy." Give members time to adjust! Be intentional about change, taking one step at a time and reviewing every change. If something isn't working, *Don't Do It Anymore!* Remind people often that worship is part of your congregation's outreach. Create a climate of joy. Praise members often for their commitment to and their part in creating joyful, uplifting worship. And finally, pray more often!

Bob Mooney has been at Messiah Lutheran Church in Yorba Linda, California, for the past ten years. He served three years as the associate pastor and the last seven as the senior pastor. His first parish was in Scottsdale, Arizona. Bob completed his B.S. in psychology at California Lutheran University and received his M.Div. at Pacific Lutheran Theological Seminary at Berkeley, California.

Cheryl Driver served on the staff of Messiah as organist and director of music from 1976 to 1995. She has worked in church music since 1968 as organist at many U.S. Army Chapels in Germany and the U.S. She earned a bachelor of music degree in composition from California State University at Fullerton in 1988. She composed a choral anthem, "I Have Heard Your Prayer," for the dedication of Messiah's new sanctuary in 1991.

Contemporary Worship Or...

LITURGICAL	PRAYER AND PRAISE	
Definition:		
formal	informal	c.
lectionary	topical	con
textual	oral	aural
sacramental	musical	presenta
Word and Table	Praise and Worship	topical
UM Book of Worship		dramas
UM Hymnal	praise chorus book	chorus or none
historic continuity	modern	cultural
cerebral	emotional	informative—introduce people to Jesus
old mainline (UMC)	new mainline (Baptist)	independent
Source:		
tradition	contemporary music	television
Audience:		
churched believers	churched believers	seekers
churched seekers	churched seekers	churched seekers
	unconnected believers	unconnected believers
Role of Congregation:		
congregational participation	congregational participation	audience
congregation as liturgists	congregation as choir	
Setting and Environment:		
sanctuary	auditorium	theater
pulpit	lectern/PA system	stool/wireless mike
font	pool	projection system
table	table	stage
pews	flexible seating	theater seating
Sunday morning	Sunday A.M., P.M. Wednesday P.M.	Saturday P.M. Thursday P.M.
Leaders:		
pastor	teacher	worship team, speaker, band, band leader, lighting director, drama director/team, singers, choreographer, dancers
music leader	worship leader (musician)	
choir	instrumentalists: pianists to full orchestra	
Shape of Service:		
entrance	worship (singing and praying)	thematic: shape based on theme
proclamation with communion	teaching	
thanksgiving with communion		
sending forth		

	PRAYER AND PRAISE	SEEKER
UMH #89 *"Joyful, Joyful"*	UMH #123 *"El Shaddai"*	UMH #278 *"Come Sunday"*
communal	praise and worship songs	depends on audience: rock, country, rhythm and blues
hymns	some hymns	
choir and congregation	leader and congregation	leaders (congregation as audience)
organ and piano	percussion instruments	percussion and tape
UM Hymnal	chorus books	overhead projector
lowest cost	higher cost	highest cost

Preaching:

lectionary based	follow one book	thematic
exegetical	expository	explanatory
eucharistic	didactic	didactic
pastor as priest	pastor	pastor as guide
style: transparent	style: personality	style: personality

Variables:

degree of formality	singing 15 minutes to 1 hour	dress based on audience
textual or oral	planned spontaneity	offering invitation
role of choir	songbook vs. overhead projector	
frequency of communion	number/type of musical instruments	
use of bulletins		

Issues:

too textual	musical integrity	lack of congregation participation
focus on ear	focus on heart	focus on eye
tyranny of tradition	tyranny of contemporary	tyranny of culture
fear of change	personality cult	personality cult
ignorance of tradition	superficial/simplistic	worship as commodity
	materialistic	fragmented audiences
	materialistic	"not worship"

Compiled by Andy and Sally Langford from a variety of sources

Part 2

SPIRITED-TRADITIONAL WORSHIP

*Spirited-Traditional worship services
maintain the beauty, dignity, and order of liturgical worship
while adding appropriate contemporary elements.
Spirited emphasizes energy and celebration.
Traditional reminds us of our ties with
past generations of believers.*

How to Blend Contemporary and Traditional Elements Without Offending Everyone

KAREN REYNOLDS

A change in worship without a process will bring out all kinds of offense! It would be like changing the noon meal my farming parents have eaten every Sunday in their fifty years of marriage. Dinner is at 12:00 noon, and the menu consists of roast beef, mashed potatoes, gravy, corn, and baking powder biscuits. If you were to suddenly change their meal, you would be in for a fight. And I wouldn't blame them. As we plan worship, we set the table for God's people. When the need arises to change the menu, we tell people why and help them develop a taste for other things. And that begins by answering a few important questions.

The first question is, "Why change how we worship?" That question ultimately leads to additional questions, such as "What is worship?" and "Who is worship for?" I have often sought answers to these foundational questions as our congregation's worship life has changed.

Why change? The style of worship has always changed. For example, most of us would feel out of place in the ancient Hebrew church. (Attend a synagogue service to sense what this means.) The language would be foreign, and the tonal structure of the music would feel, at best, very awkward. The message would still be about a loving God who forgives sin—but I wouldn't understand it. Many of us still expect people today to feel at home in a church filled with organ music and foreign expressions like "collect of the day" or "introit." However, none of these things are indigenous to our culture. In other words, these things make many people feel like they are in a foreign country. People then begin to feel that God is foreign and inaccessible. The question is not, "Should we change?" but, "What needs to change to be relevant to people in this culture, at this time in history?"

What is worship? (Or, we could ask, what is not worship?) Worship is not a style or a form. We learn from Jesus in John 4 that worship happens in spirit and truth. Worship is at the heart of the believer who adores God for who he is and what he has done. When we plan worship, our job is to facilitate the meeting between God and the people of God. We want to give people tools to communicate and express their love and praise of God.

Some have argued that only certain tools or actions are allowed in worship. But what makes one instrument more worthy of God than another? What makes one style of music more worthy of God than another in any given community or place in Christian time? Personal taste? Childhood experience? Church policy manuals? Theological pronouncements? Authoritative prayer books?

Our music, texts, and instruments find their value in worship as God uses them to transform the hearts and lives of God's people. If God were concerned about the value of the vessel, why use spit and mud as a sign of healing for a blind man? Or why use bread and wine or water as signs for our most important Christian practices? Or why allow Jesus to be born as a mere human being? God has always reached into our world by using familiar things so that we could acknowledge him and commune with him.

For whom is worship? It is for God and for the one who worships. Not either/or but both/and. Our lens is always Jesus: "Let us fix our eyes on Jesus" (Heb. 12:2*a* NIV). As we adore and praise God by focusing through Jesus, God appears to us. God says that he dwells in the praises of his people. In 2 Chronicles 5 we see the picture of Israel singing and praising God. When they sang, the glory of the Lord filled the temple with a cloud. On Pentecost, as the disciples were worshiping, the Holy Spirit came in a mighty rush of wind. Today, God still comes to God's people as they praise him. And when he does, it changes their lives and gives them renewed life.

Having answered those preliminary questions, how do we then blend the best of past practices and the best of present imagination about the God whom we worship? Here are some practical suggestions:

1. Pray for God's vision and begin with baby steps.

2. Begin listening to tapes of contemporary Christian music. Some churches offer a tape or CD library so that guests and members can check out music and become familiar with the styles and lyrics.

3. Introduce the congregation to contemporary music by having a soloist or choir sing a contemporary song during worship. Make sure that the style of contemporary music fits the overall "feel," or "climate" of the service.

4. Teach the singers and instrumentalists how to lead the worship by leading the congregation in the singing of hymns and songs.

5. Begin to develop a sing-a-long style (the congregation sings along with the leader or choir on the songs).

6. Help people understand the difference between the method and the message. Remind them that while the method may change, the message stays the same.

7. Teach about worship in Bible studies or youth and adult classes, and cultivate an attitude of worship.

8. Put two to four songs together in a medley, mixing well-loved hymns and some contemporary worship choruses.

9. Invite the congregation to experiment with a blended style of worship for six months and then give them the chance to evaluate it.

10. Understand that change can be, and often is, chaotic.

11. Study other churches and how they faced the same issues.

12. Spend time and money educating the choir, instrumentalists, and other leaders in the area of worship, worship leadership, and contemporary expressions of worship.

13. Be excellent in everything you do.

14. If you currently use only the organ, start incorporating some different instruments. To use songs with a pop style sound, find a good drummer.

15. If you are the worship leader, don't be afraid to lead.

These suggestions will not eliminate all the opposition or discomfort. Remember to be sensitive to those who are not pleased by the change. Remember that relationships are very important. When people are angry about a different style of worship, don't fight or flee, but think of ways to be clear and gentle as you express your vision for worship. Realize that there will be a price to pay, but that the benefits will be beyond your imagination. When people hear the gospel sung and spoken in ways that they may not have heard before, they will respond. Not because of what you have done, but because of what they are finally hearing. For "faith comes by hearing, and hearing by the Word of God" (Rom. 10:17 KJV).

Karen Reynolds is the minister of music at Community of Grace in Omaha, Nebraska.

Worship Is a Relationship

KENT R. HUNTER

Many horror stories about unfriendliness and coldness exist among those who travel and visit churches as guests. These stories might be summed up in a misquotation of Scripture: "Many are cold but few are frozen." As a church consultant, I frequently fill the role as a church visitor. I like to attend a church for the first time as an "undercover" guest. No one knows that I am a church analyst. I have learned to act like a visitor. I take on a timid demeanor and hesitancy and look around, indicating that I am seeing things for the first time.

My most miserable visit occurred in a church in Missouri. It is a very large church, with hundreds of people in attendance. I had trouble finding a parking spot in the crowded lot. Numerous people passed me as I made my way to the front door. There in the lobby was a guest register. I took a full five minutes putting my name in the register, seeing if anyone might come up to me and welcome me. As I entered the sanctuary, the usher was deeply engaged in a friendly conversation with one of his peers and mechanically handed me a bulletin while looking the other way. I attended worship and participated in the Lord's Supper. On the way out of church, no one spoke to me, even though the hallways were crowded with people. As I passed by the pastor at the door, he was talking with someone who was reporting that her mother was in the hospital. This church is immersed in maintenance with little sensitivity to the first-time visitor.

Wal-Mart Versus First Church

When people find Wal-Mart more friendly than your church, it is time to ask why. Note that the people at Wal-Mart, who actually want your business, provide friendly greeters. They show appreciation for your presence and your business. The reason for the sensitivity is that the people at Wal-Mart are driven by the incredible notion that you might come back!

Have you ever gone to a restaurant where you got the feeling the people were doing you a favor by taking your money? The attitude and actions of the people who serve you are a symbol of the ambiance in the equation of a pleasant dining experience.

I recently heard about a study conducted among restaurant patrons. People were asked why they go back to a restaurant or why they do not return. Over and over, people said it was because of the service. Yet, many restaurant owners think of their business with a narrow vision. They think their business is to feed people!

Sometimes church leaders get the impression that they are in the doctrine business. They think that their main job is to feed people the truth, even if they have to shove it down their throats. It is true that the Word of God never returns void. It always has some impact. The Holy Spirit is at work and the gospel is the power unto salvation. But, when we treat guests as lepers, we are tempting God! Perhaps we ought to remember that we call it a worship *service*. Is friendliness important? Twenty years of research has shown that there are two major reasons why people return to join a church they have visited: They found (1) a message relevant to their behaviors and life issues, and (2) a friendly congregation.

Who Says Your Church Is Friendly?

When we consult congregations, we conduct a diagnostic analysis prior to the on-site visit. We use several random sampling questionnaires. In one of the questionnaires, we ask longtime members what they see as the priorities for their church. We ask them to identify what makes their church unique. In just about every congregation, one of the most frequent responses is that their church is friendly. In a separate survey, we analyze the views of new members, those who have affiliated with the church three years or less. One of the questions we ask them is, "What does this church need to do to improve?" Amazingly, one of the most frequent responses is that the church needs to be more friendly!

Who is right about what to improve? The long-term members or the newcomers? All of the above is the right answer! Sure the church members are friendly—to one another! But, to the outsider, the new person, it often feels like a journey into the deep freeze.

Eight Most Productive Steps to Friendliness

1. Get an attitude. Philippians 2:5-11 says that the attitude we should have is one like that of Christ Jesus. Jesus was humble and obedient. He was a servant willing to meet people where they are instead of expecting them to come to him. Our attitudes shape our behavior. So, begin by training and teaching people to have an attitude of outreach, a sensitivity to unbelievers. Direct the members of your congregation to read materials on how to be mission-minded. Help them experience what it is like to be a visitor. Ask the leaders of your congregation to visit another church occasionally that is totally foreign to them. Ask them to go alone. You see, many Christians have forgotten what it is like to be a guest. Ask your members to occasionally put on visitor shoes and see how it feels.

2. Check the lot. If most people come by car, the parking lot (at peak times) can be a contest of nerves. When the parking lot is 80 percent full, you need more parking. Provide guest parking places near the front door, with signs designating them. Many churches have reserved parking spots by the front door—for the pastor or the choir director. So much for servanthood. Hooray for perks!

If your lot is overcrowded, initiate another worship service. Or, you can develop a L.O.V.E. Club. L.O.V.E. stands for Leave Our Vehicles Elsewhere. Teach the leadership to park in a remote lot. Or, at the very least,

provide parking attendants to help people find a spot and to give them a friendly greeting.

Also, ask whether a newcomer can identify the front door. It is amazing to find out how many churches are built with several main entrances. If a visitor comes a little late, she or he may feel that finding the front door is as confusing as a maze.

3. What does the building look like? During the 1950s, America had a baby boom. Churches, during the same period, had a building boom. Consequently, there are numerous churches around the country that look like 1950s buildings. They are simply out of date.

Just about every public building has a routine face-lift. Every airport, library, courthouse, restaurant, college, and other public buildings undergo remodeling from time to time to fix what is broken, use colors that are popular, and provide architectural changes that are reflective of the era.

Does your building reflect an old, out-of-date, irrelevant going-out-of-business ministry? If so, you are communicating something that is inappropriate for God, who is alive, dynamic, and fresh as today's news. Take no offense at this remark: To you, your building wears like an old shoe. To a guest, however, it looks worn out and tacky.

4. Greet people at the door. "Anyone can be a greeter," said Jane. "We'll just divide up the congregation alphabetically, provide assignments to all the members, and let them know that it is their Sunday to be greeters. At least that is something everyone can do!" Greeting, however, is not a "job" you do when your name comes up. It is a ministry. Not every personality or gift mix is appropriate for greeting. Develop a core group of people who see this as their ministry. They should concentrate on this ministry as perhaps the only ministry in which they are involved. They should be trained, equipped, and committed to following up on those who are guests. They should serve regularly, not just once a year. If they serve on a regular basis, they can improve their skills and get to know the members. This will in turn help them to identify guests and learn better ways to greet them.

Most of all, provide greeters who are incognito commandos. These people serve as plainclothed, undercover greeters. Their sole responsibility on Sunday morning is to wander the halls and hang out at the front door, to be prepared to spend time with guests, direct them to the sanctuary, nursery, church office, restrooms, and sit with them during worship. They, too, should be trained for this important ministry.

5. **Can guests find the restrooms?** Does the inside of your church building read like a public building? Is it visitor-friendly? Does it show that you expect guests? Can guests find the restroom without hiring a guide or purchasing a road map? What about the church office? Can they locate the sanctuary? Where do they go to register a child in Sunday school? Do they know about adult classes? Is the nursery visible and accessible? What about public telephones? There should be signs everywhere inside the church, just like at the hospital or airport. There will be those in the congregation who will object to all signs. Those people are telling you something. They identify the church as "our" home—not as an outreach center. They need an attitude adjustment based on a review of the New Testament.

6. **Provide a high impact worship bulletin.** Your worship bulletin should be readable and comprehensible to a fifth grade level, unchurched person. It should be well printed and presented. You are presenting information to people who read *U.S.A. Today*. Thus there should be use of graphics for right brain, conceptually oriented people. Begin with a welcome paragraph. You can imagine what it is like to be a guest who opens the bulletin, and, at the upper left-hand corner of the first page, reads a paragraph explaining that last week's income was $850. The weekly need is $950. The shortfall was $100. An unchurched guest might reflect, "Let's not join here; the place is going bankrupt!"

Lay out the worship service in your bulletin so that anyone can follow it. Do not use three different hymnals, the worship folder, and an insert—unless you are only reaching out to jugglers.

7. **Teach worship leaders to smile.** All too often, the choir sings with facial expressions that make one wonder if their underwear is too tight. Or, the ushers look like they were all baptized in vinegar. You can smile and sing at the same time. In fact, you can even preach about the serious consequences of sin and smile—because if you do not offer grace, above all that God is love, then you have only offered half of the gospel. A large portion of communication is nonverbal. If all you communicate is doom and gloom, guests and members can experience that by sitting at home and reading the Sunday newspaper.

8. **Let guests know you appreciate their visit.** Provide a follow-up call by telephone, a letter, and a visit. It is best that the visit be

done by a layperson, not a pastor or staff person. In the mind of most secular people, pastors or staff are paid to do that. But, when a lay volunteer comes to visit, it communicates genuine appreciation. Visits after worship should be made within twenty-four hours, and preferably, the same day.

A church in the Seattle area has a budget item of $600 per year for its pie ministry. My first reaction was, when analyzing the budget, "That is a lot of money for pies!" But, then I learned that ordinary people take these pies to people who have visited the church. The pie is freshly baked and delivered warm from the oven! As I interviewed numerous new members of that church, I was amazed to discover how many of them indicated that they were impressed with the friendliness of the congregation and specifically mentioned the pie as an expression of that kindness.

Signs and Pie

Worship in the church is not about signs to the restrooms and pies to the visitors, about techniques and public relations. The church is all about sin and grace. It is all about hope and life. It is all about Jesus and the eternal comfort of God's Spirit. The cost of discipleship, however, does not give your church an excuse for being sour or unfriendly as you retell the good news story.

Kent R. Hunter is the president of the Church Growth Center in Corunna, Indiana. He serves as a consultant to churches and has written numerous books including, *Foundations for Church Growth: Biblical Basics for the Local Church* and *Moving the Church into Action*. Audio resources include *Twenty Things Every Greeter Should Know* and *There Must Be 50 Ways to Improve Your Worship Bulletin*. Kent is senior editor of the magazine *Strategies for Today's Leader* and is heard on Christian radio as "The Church Doctor."

Worship Is an Environment

WALT KALLESTAD

On my ordination day, Mom whispered something in my ear that has affected everything that I have been a part of in ministry. She said, "Always let the people see Jesus." Mom knew what was most important. When it comes to people visiting a church, how is it possible to always make sure that they see Jesus and experience his unconditional love and unlimited peace?

Many churches, sadly, have symptoms of "koinonitis." As Dr. C. Peter Wagner explains, "koinonitis" comes from the Greek word *koinonia,* meaning "fellowship." Certainly, fellowship is essential and healthy for every congregation. But Wagner tells us that when congregations value fellowship with one another at the expense of reaching out to others, koinonia becomes the deadly disease koinonitis—the disease of locking others out of the church.

When I came to my present calling I dreamed of creating a congregation that warmly welcomed all who came. At that time the congregation offered one service—a traditional, Lutheran, liturgical service. I believed that we could make that style of worship more relational and inviting for newcomers (even though I knew we would ultimately need to offer contemporary services in the near future if we truly wanted to reach secular people). To do this we set about creating a climate of hospitality that welcomed people as they entered the worship facility. But I also decided that intentional steps would be taken to make the worship environment hospitable and relational, rather than monastic.

So here are some steps for building a relational environment in the worship service:

1. Change the prelude. Instead of using low-key organ music, which sets a climate for contemplation, play up-tempo, inspirational music tapes that create an atmosphere of energy and allow for conversation. New generations of people are more likely to prepare for worship, not through silence, but through conversation with others, sharing concerns, joys, and hopes. A contemplative person in public worship is very much the exception and almost always someone who has been long on the Christian journey, rather than an unchurched guest.

2. Greet people when they arrive. As the pastor, I welcome people when they come into the worship center, and shake their hands or hug them when they leave. I let people know how important their presence is to God and to our church family. A smile and a welcome from the visible leader prepares people so that when I present my message they are more receptive. After that modest change, the pastor(s) may want to walk up and down the aisles greeting people before worship begins to establish an inviting environment.

3. Greet the congregation with an uplifting "Good Morning!" After opening the worship service with a dynamic anthem I offer people an enthusiastic, "Good Morning!" I then repeat the verse that my mom and dad spoke every day of every week of every month of every year while I was growing up: "This is the day the LORD has made. [I will] rejoice and be glad in it" (Ps. 118:24 NIV). After speaking those inspirational words, invite everyone to sing the words. It is amazing how the atmosphere and attitudes brighten up.

4. Greet the people around you. After welcoming everyone, invite the congregation to give the warmest, friendliest welcome they can imagine to the people around them. Encourage people to give a handshake, a hug, or a spirited "hello" to the people beside them, behind them, in front of them, and across from them.

5. Offer guests a special word of welcome. Once the people greet one another, again remind them of how great it is that they are in church. Share a special word of welcome with the guests. Announce that the ushers will be distributing a welcome folder. Explain that the welcome folder is meant to help people get to know one another better and to help us continue to build a friendly church. Every person is asked to take a name tag, provided in the folder, in order to help them connect names with faces. Once they have filled out the welcome folder (name, address, phone number, member or guest), they can be encouraged to pass it down the row so that others can use it and get to know the people next to them. (This has also been an excellent way for getting the names of our first-time guests.)

6. Sing a hymn. Following that time of welcome (which actually only takes two to three minutes) sing an inspirational hymn. An uplifting melody sets the right climate for experiencing God's good news.

7. Explain the worship service for newcomers. Throughout the worship experience carefully explain everything in order to include newcomers. Tell them where to find the hymnals. Share with them the page numbers or hymn numbers. Continually invite guests to participate by including them in the action. Those who have been to worship regularly know what to do and when to do it. But those who are visiting for the first time may find themselves confused by all the page turning, standing, and sitting. However, they will feel embraced when the worship leaders graciously help them follow along. By assuming that everybody has "been there and done that" we send a subtle message that this place is for members only.

8. Greet guests again at the end of the service. End your worship service the way you began it—warmly greeting one another. Encourage people as they leave to say "Hi" to someone they've never met before or to share a smile with a new friend. People need to be reminded in a positive, motivating way about the value and worth of those around them. We shouldn't assume that people will naturally mingle. We need to encourage it.

9. Share food and fellowship. Encourage people to stop by a special area for some coffee, punch, and doughnuts after the service. Gathering around food creates a friendly atmosphere. Try to provide a place where guests would be treated better than they would be at the Ritz Carlton or Disneyland. Have someone pour the coffee or juice and hand it to people with a smile. Have hosts and hostesses serve the snacks rather than simply setting the food out on the table. The smile and friendly service make all the difference.

I encourage you to be creative as you seek to build a worship environment. As "little Christs," we intentionally work on living out our Christianity—starting in worship and then moving into the outmost parts of the world.

And always remember how much joy a friendly church brings to the heart of God and to the heart of God's people!

Walt Kallestad is the senior pastor of Community Church of Joy—an Evangelical Lutheran Church in America congregation located in Glendale, Arizona. He has written several books, including *Entertainment Evangelism: Taking the Church Public* **(Abingdon Press, 1996),** *The Everyday, Anytime Guide to Christian Leadership, Total Quality Ministry,* **and** *The Everyday, Anytime Guide to Prayer* **(Augsburg Fortress, 1995), and** *Wake Up Your Dreams* **(Zondervan Publishing House, 1996).**

Better Bulletins for Worship

KENT R. HUNTER

Joe walks into a church, sits down, and begins to read the bulletin. "The AWL group will meet at the usual time this week at the DCE's house. We will discuss the use of the Kyrie in worship. All members and visitors are most welcome." Don't believe it!

Key to Communication

One of the most visible, valuable pieces of communication regularly put in the hands of members and guests is the worship bulletin. How do you judge the effectiveness of your bulletin? First, the quality of your bulletin should be based on the size of your church, reflected by the number of people in worship. The larger church can, and should, produce a much better bulletin than the smaller church. Likewise, the intimate smaller church should not feel that it has to produce a customized four-color bulletin with photos and expensive fonts.

As churches grow larger, there are many

changes that should take place. In fact, one of the common roadblocks to church vitality comes when a church grows larger but continues to act like a smaller church. As a church grows, communication is one of the several important areas of change that should take place.

Communication in the larger church should become more intentional, sophisticated, formal, repeated, and should be offered through a variety of media—including a well-presented bulletin. However, in the smaller church, the need is not so acute. In a smaller church, communication is more verbal, spontaneous, and informal. In fact, that is one of the joys and benefits of a smaller church.

In the very small church, there is probably little justification for having a bulletin at all. This is true, especially if (1) the bivocational pastor spends time producing the entire bulletin; (2) the cost of the equipment is a burden to the budget; (3) the church has an overhead projector or a bulletin board that can be used for information sharing; and

(4) the fewer activities of a small church can be announced verbally.

Quality Impact

The first impression and overall "feel" of the bulletin is very important. You have only one opportunity to make a first impression. People do judge a book—and a bulletin—by its cover!

There are several first-impression issues that are important. First, consider the quality and crispness of the printing. We live in the era of desktop publishing. What used to come out of a professional print shop or a bulletin publisher can now be produced by seventh grade students at home. Crispness depends on a number of factors. On what equipment do you type the bulletin? How is the master prepared? What kind of a machine do you use to make copies? What is the quality of the paper that you use?

Second, the use of graphics is important, particularly for people who were raised on *Sesame Street* or who spent time in *Mister Rogers' Neighborhood*. These are conceptually oriented people who are used to an image of a woman on the door, rather than a sign that says "Ladies' Room."

Third, white space is important in margins, between items, and around the graphics. The church secretary who puts the material of the bulletin "border to border" on the page was probably born before 1945 and wants to save paper.

Fourth, the generic publishing house stock is helpful for smaller churches. But, if a church worships with over 350 to 400 persons per week, I suggest developing a personalized bulletin that changes seasonally or with message (sermon series) themes.

Visitor-Friendly

Lloyd stood up at the meeting and was about to speak. The same thought was in everyone's mind. Whatever it was he wanted to say, it probably had to do with money. "I don't see why we waste all that paper Sunday after Sunday. We print out the entire worship service and even the words to the hymns. Meanwhile, the hymnal sits there in the pew and we never use it. What did we get all those hymnals for, anyway?"

The answer to Lloyd's questions, whatever it might be, is not "we got the hymnals for the visitors!" The typical hymnal is a nightmare of frustration for the average guest. Consequently, many churches are wisely providing an easier, single-source, chronological way to follow the worship service. That is usually provided in the bulletin.

There are many ways you can make your worship bulletin more user-friendly. Here are some of them:

1. Avoid code words. Look out for in-house jargon that tells visitors they are neither expected nor wanted.

2. Begin the bulletin with material that provides a welcome to guests and members.

3. In the use of graphics, avoid a picture or drawing of the building. (This applies to stationery, as well.) Too many people already have the unbiblical notion that the church is bricks and mortar. Use pictures of people. My favorite bulletin cover is from Grace Community Church in Toledo, Ohio. Susan Coss, an artist and member, took pictures of the members and then drew a caricature/collage of the faces of some of the members for the cover of the worship bulletin. Every year, she takes more pictures and makes another

cover. This clearly communicates that the church is people.

4. Avoid publicizing weekly financial giving in the worship bulletin to persons who have no concept of the costs of building a church. Financial information is "family" business and should not be communicated during a worship service. This is especially true at this time in history when secular people have many doubts about the financial integrity and motivation of religious organizations. (On the other hand, don't err with the opposite attitude that church finances are *always* a "private" matter.)

5. Prepare the content of the bulletin so that a first-time guest can understand it. If you really want a good evaluation, pass out copies of your worship bulletin at a local beauty salon, cocktail lounge, or Little League baseball game among those who do not attend church. Ask the people to circle anything that does not make sense to them. It may be a humbling experience.

6. Avoid loose pages, also known as "ecclesiastical inserts." They simply fall out too much and frustrate people—especially visitors. Staple the bulletins together in the center.

7. When you list the church address and phone number, put the name of the person who will answer the phone when someone calls. People today are relationally connected and are much less concerned with communicating with an institution. Guests will feel more comfortable if they have the name of the person speaking.

8. When the sermon or message is listed, put the name of the preacher next to it. This is especially helpful if there is more than one pastor on staff listed in the bulletin.

9. Translate ancient church language to communicate with the twenty-first century secular mission field. Most people do not understand Latin. Avoid sexist language whenever possible. Call the sermon a message, the hymn a song, the visitor a guest, and the benediction a good word from God. Work on translating words like "Amen," "blessing," and "grace." Tell guests they do not have to feel obligated to give to the offering. If you provide Bibles in the pews, offer page numbers. Assume nothing!

10. Advertise next week's message. Bring guests back.

11. Put your mission statement on every bulletin.

12. Consider using recycled paper to show concern for the environment.

13. Identify the editor of the bulletin. This will help people to know where they can go to respond to something in the bulletin.

14. Before the bulletin is printed, have three people look it over very carefully for errors. Each of these three people should not include the person who typed it. For every one hundred people in worship, eighty-five of them read the bulletin. The other fifteen proofread the bulletin!

The Cafeteria Church

In the larger church that worships with more than five hundred in multiple services, it is helpful to develop each worship service as a distinctive congregation. One of the values of a large church is that it can provide choices. In a complex community with several people groups, the larger church can segment the style of its worship services to reach different people groups.

To help develop each worship service as a distinctive congregation give each service a name. Develop a profile description of that worship service and print it in the bulletin designed for that specific service. Provide a different bulletin for each worship service. It may be identified by entirely different artwork that reflects the theme and style of the service. It may also be printed in a different color.

As your congregation develops outreach strategies to reach your community, target the different groups in your area by defining each niche through style, music, setting, day, and time of each worship service.

Develop a worship team, ushers, and musicians for each worship service. In some congregations, with multiple staffs, different staff people consistently preach at specific worship services. This is a multicellular approach to a larger church. It recognizes the reality that larger churches are not simply a larger form of a smaller church, but are really a different kind of church, which reflects a conglomerate of smaller congregations within a larger entity.

Start more worship services as outreach strategies, targeted to specific groups within your community. By doing this, you will be pursuing one of the most productive church growth principles: church planting. But, you will be doing it in one of the most cost-effective ways: planting a church within a church.

Worship Bulletin Board

In this age of electronic technology, prepare for the day when just about every church will have an electronic billboard. It may not replace the worship bulletin filled with announcements people take with them. But, the electronic billboard will probably display the worship service in the future. This will allow people to focus on the service, leaving their hands free for worship and praise.

Kent R. Hunter is president of the Church Growth Center in Corunna, Indiana. He serves as a consultant for churches and has written numerous books, including, *Foundations for Church Growth: Biblical Basics for the Local Church* and *Moving the Church into Action*. Audio resources include *Twenty Things Every Greeter Should Know* and *There Must Be 50 Ways to Improve Your Worship Bulletin*. Kent is the senior editor of the magazine *Strategies for Today's Leader* and is heard on Christian radio as "The Church Doctor."

Characteristics of Spirited-Traditional Choral Music

BEV ALTOPP

1. Spirited-Traditional choral music, because it leans toward a contemporary sound, generally uses today's language and tends to focus on current subject matter. Classical pieces often use "King James" English, and while beautiful and moving, tend not to be as personal and "warm" as more contemporary choral songs.

2. The music uses a less constrictive rhythm and tempo. Syncopation plays a vital part in communicating energy.

3. Spirited-Traditional choral music does not use four-part harmony consistently. Classical music will often utilize a lot of counterpoint and four-part harmonies. Spirited-Traditional songs, on the other hand, commonly use solos with backup choral parts and unison female and/or male melodies. Not as much is written for high sopranos and low basses. Three-part harmony gives a tighter sound, thus making it more contemporary. When using music with traditional four-part harmony, you may want to consolidate parts to give it a more contemporary flavor.

4. Much of Spirited-Traditional choral music is derived from songs written for solo contemporary artists and arranged for choral groups.

5. Spirited-Traditional choral music lends itself to the use of a full rhythm section. The band adds a contemporary flare and energizes the singers. When searching for choral music, look for arrangements that include a chord chart written above the accompaniment line. This indicates that the song can be played by a rhythm section above the accompaniment line. This indicates improvising. Classical music tends to restrict rhythms and leaves very little room for personal interpretation.

6. Spirited-Traditional choral music utilizes a strong hook (a melody and/or chord progression that recurs throughout the piece) that catches the listener's attention. The form—verse, chorus, verse, chorus, bridge, chorus—allows the lyric to become memorable quickly.

In summary, when choosing music for a blended service, look for choral music that:

- Makes use of great melody lines
- Incorporates interesting rhythms
- Utilizes strong and prevalent lyrics
- Offers interesting harmonizations
- Uses a variety of tempos (contemporary has to do with style, not speed)
- Maintains a heart-tugging partnership between lyric, melody, and rhythm

The following publishing companies offer music that fits the above description:

Brentwood Music, 1-800-333-9000
Lillenas Publishing Company, 1-800-877-0700
Word Music, Inc., 1-800-933-9673
Spectra Music, 1-800-365-7732

Bev Altopp serves as choral director at Community Church of Joy, in Glendale, Arizona. She is also an accomplished songwriter, having written several musical productions for the congregation along with drama director Terey Summers.

Resource Kit 1
SPIRITED–TRADITIONAL WORSHIP

Notes: This resource kit contains *two sample worship services*, *two sample sermons*, and *a chart listing several Spirited-Traditional choral pieces*. This list is by no means exhaustive, but should provide a good introduction to Spirited-Traditional choral music. The choral numbers included in the sample worship services can be found in that list.

The choruses suggested in the sample worship services are listed in the chorus chart provided in the Resource Kit in part 3. All choruses in that chart marked by an asterisk would be appropriate for a Spirited-Traditional format.

Small group numbers cited in the sample worship services can be found in the charts in the Resource Kit in part 4.

For the hymns used in these services consult any denominational hymnal.

SPIRITED–TRADITIONAL SERVICE

Sermon Series

Getting to Know the God Who Loves You—
PART ONE

Getting to Know the God Who Guides You— The Story of Joseph

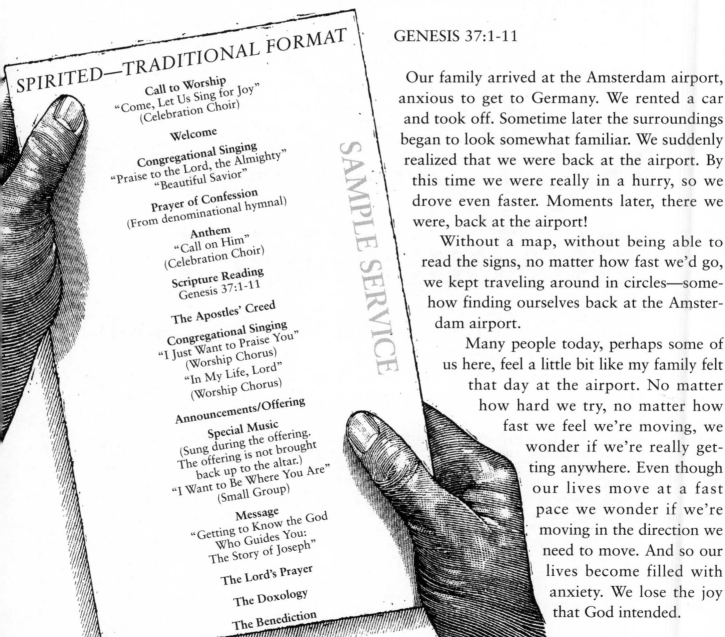

SPIRITED—TRADITIONAL FORMAT

Call to Worship
"Come, Let Us Sing for Joy"
(Celebration Choir)

Welcome

Congregational Singing
"Praise to the Lord, the Almighty"
"Beautiful Savior"

Prayer of Confession
(From denominational hymnal)

Anthem
"Call on Him"
(Celebration Choir)

Scripture Reading
Genesis 37:1-11

The Apostles' Creed

Congregational Singing
"I Just Want to Praise You"
(Worship Chorus)
"In My Life, Lord"
(Worship Chorus)

Announcements/Offering

Special Music
(Sung during the offering.
The offering is not brought
back up to the altar.)
"I Want to Be Where You Are"
(Small Group)

Message
"Getting to Know the God
Who Guides You:
The Story of Joseph"

The Lord's Prayer

The Doxology

The Benediction

SAMPLE SERVICE

GENESIS 37:1-11

Our family arrived at the Amsterdam airport, anxious to get to Germany. We rented a car and took off. Sometime later the surroundings began to look somewhat familiar. We suddenly realized that we were back at the airport. By this time we were really in a hurry, so we drove even faster. Moments later, there we were, back at the airport!

Without a map, without being able to read the signs, no matter how fast we'd go, we kept traveling around in circles—somehow finding ourselves back at the Amsterdam airport.

Many people today, perhaps some of us here, feel a little bit like my family felt that day at the airport. No matter how hard we try, no matter how fast we feel we're moving, we wonder if we're really getting anywhere. Even though our lives move at a fast pace we wonder if we're moving in the direction we need to move. And so our lives become filled with anxiety. We lose the joy that God intended.

As we begin our series, "Getting to Know the God Who Loves You," we're first going to focus on getting to know the God who guides us. We will look at the story of Joseph and see how God guided him. But before we talk about it, let's pray together.

1. God Gives Us Dreams

Joseph had a dream. It was a crazy dream. Joseph dreamed that as he and his brothers were gathering bundles of wheat, his bundle stood up and his brothers' bundles bowed down to his.

Joseph had another dream. He dreamed that the stars, the moon, and the sun bowed down to him. Another crazy dream. But a dream that would eventually save the life of his family, save a nation, and spare the people of God. As we take a closer look at this story we see that one of the ways in which God guides us is through dreams. God plants dreams in our hearts.

Before this world existed there was chaos, formlessness—it was void. But God had a dream. He dreamed of plants and animals, trees and flowers. He dreamed of people whom he could love. God said, "Let there be light. . . . Let there be land and animals . . . and plants and people." Out of nothingness God spoke something into being. And as people created by God, you and I are also given that special ability to dream. To consider what is not yet there. To imagine what hasn't been. What might be.

In the book of Acts, Peter quotes from the prophet Joel and speaks about the last days—the days in which we live right now. He said, "'In the last days, God says, I will pour out my Spirit on all people. Your sons and daughters will prophesy, your young [people] will see visions, your old [people] will dream dreams'" (Acts 2:17 NIV).

Do you consider yourselves young people? I'm edging out of that category, I'm afraid. Young people will see visions.

Do you consider yourselves old people? You will have dreams.

By God's visions and dreams I don't think God is talking about a multicolor movie production in our minds. Not a dream that we would have while asleep. By visions and dreams I believe that God will plant in our minds and our hearts new ideas. Imaginings. Concepts that aren't yet there, that we haven't considered before.

Remember, though, that there is a difference between a dream and a scheme. A schemer plans and devises opportunities for himself or herself. The vision is launched for personal gain, often at the expense of another person, or at least for the sake of personal control. Schemers often arise during times when there are no youthful visionaries and mature dreamers.

A dream, on the other hand, is something that God gives us. It's a picture, an idea, an imaginative concept that can help other people. And ultimately it brings glory to God.

Mother Teresa saw the poorest of the poor strewn out on the streets of Calcutta. She saw the destitute and the dying, and God gave her a dream. God gave her a dream to pick these people up. To bring hope and healing to their lives. And through that dream she has touched millions of people around the world. That's a dream from God.

God wants so desperately to bring his dreams to your heart. To give you ideas and imaginations that you haven't considered before. Perhaps you're facing a roadblock. Perhaps you're facing a problem or a challenge, and you need to make a decision. Take time to dream. Step back out of the intensity of that decision. Give the Lord your thoughts and ideas. And God will give you his dreams.

So God guides us by giving us a dream. He plants dreams in our hearts.

2. God Guides Us by Walking with Us into Our Dreams

When Joseph shared his dream with his brothers, his struggles began. He had started out on the wrong foot. The Bible tells us that Joseph was his father's favorite son. As Tommy Smothers used to say to his brother, Dick, "Mom always liked you best." That's what Joseph's brothers said to him. "Dad always liked you best!" And it was true. In fact, to show his favor, Joseph's father gave him a beautiful multicolored coat.

His brothers were jealous. They despised Joseph, and he became the family snitch. If his brothers did something wrong, he was the first to tell his father. Not the kind of sibling you'd like to have, is he?

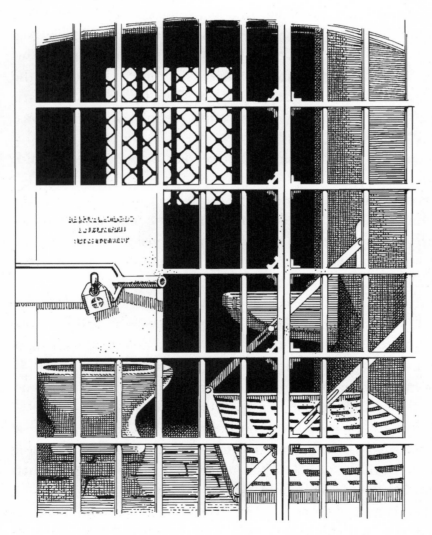

Well, to make matters worse, Joseph received the dreams, and he shared them with his brothers. That turned their jealousy and envy into rage and hatred toward him. At the first opportunity they bound him with a rope and threw him into a well. But, instead of killing him, they sold him as a slave. They took that multicolored coat and dipped it into animal's blood, then went to their father and said, "Joseph has been killed."

And that was just the beginning of Joseph's problems.

After Joseph was sold into slavery he worked for Potiphar, one of the most powerful leaders in Egypt. Potiphar's wife made advances toward Joseph and tried to seduce him. Joseph ran. So Potiphar's wife cried, "Rape!" Immediately Joseph was thrown into prison, the door was slammed shut, and the key was thrown away.

Now, if you were Joseph, if you were in that situation, wouldn't you say, "Lord, if this is your dream for me, I don't want it"?

Haven't you felt that way? You were walking in the way that you thought God was leading you. It didn't seem to be going so well so you asked, "Lord, what's happening here? Where are you?"

Genesis 39 tells us in at least two places that "The Lord was with Joseph." Verse 3, for example, says: "His master saw that the Lord was with [Joseph]" (NIV).

In the midst of his problems, in the middle of that jail cell, Joseph sensed that the Lord was with him, walking with him every moment. And the Lord is with you. Even in those times when you don't sense his presence, the Lord is with you.

Joseph, instead of turning sour and bitter toward God, used his talents. Eventually the warden put him in charge of all the prisoners. He was given a responsibility and an opportunity to serve.

This sense of God's presence is apparent in the story about a missionary who was trying to find a village in Africa. On this journey he became lost. He couldn't find his way. Eventually a villager found him and said to him, "Sir, come with me. I know the path to the village." So the missionary trusted him and followed behind. The villager used a machete to cut through all the vegetation. After awhile the missionary grew frustrated and said, "I'm sorry, but I thought you told me you knew the path to the village." The villager turned and said, "I am the path. Follow me."

Jesus says the same to you and to me. "I am the path. I am the way. I am the truth. I am the life. Follow me." Jesus invites us into a special relationship with him and a friendship whereby we can know him. We can follow him. He can guide us through each and every troubled path.

One of the ways that he does that is through his Word. The Bible says, "Thy word is a lamp unto my feet and a light unto my path" (Ps. 119:105 KJV). God takes us each step of the way.

Proverbs says, "Trust in the LORD with all your heart." Trust in him! "Do not lean on your own understanding. In all your ways acknowledge him, and he will make your paths straight" (Prov. 3:5-6 NIV).

God also walks with us through our dreams, which are received through prayer, and not through our self-interested scheming. For example, a man wanted to go on a diet. And he was so committed to making it work that he even changed his driving route to the office. In the past, he'd always stopped off at the bakery for a box of treats. But he was now determined to never go into that bakery again.

Things were going along pretty well until one day he walked into the office with a huge box of delicious looking sweets. His coworkers began to tease him about it when he said, "Wait a minute. You'll never believe what happened. On my way to work this morning I accidentally drove by the bakery. I thought to myself, this must be God's will. So I prayed, 'Lord, if it's your will that I stop at the bakery today, I pray that a parking spot will open up right in front of the bakery door.' And sure enough, the eighth time around the block, a spot opened up!"

Prayer is more than playing games with God and twisting God's arm to get our way. Prayer is listening to God. Listening for those dreams. Listening for God to speak to us throughout the day. As we face challenges and decisions we need guidance. God will speak to us through prayer.

So God promises to not only plant dreams in our hearts but to walk with us in the midst of the dreams, guiding us through his Word and prayer.

3. God Turns Nightmares into Dreams Come True

That's exactly what happened to Joseph. After Joseph sat in prison for many years, the Pharaoh, the great leader of Egypt, had a dream that he could not interpret. Someone remembered that Joseph could interpret dreams, so Pharaoh called on Joseph to tell him the meaning of the dream. Joseph told him that the dream was a warning to Pharaoh that there would be seven years of feast followed by seven years of famine. God was letting him know in advance so that he could be prepared. Pharaoh was so impressed that he put Joseph in charge of the whole project of saving food for the famine. Joseph was now second in command to the Pharaoh.

If you understand Middle Eastern culture you'll know that a Jew ruling in Egypt is rather amazing. And he was in charge of all operations. Under Joseph's direction the people of Egypt stockpiled food during the seven years of feast. Then the famine hit. It was devastating. Soon the people had to come to Joseph for the food that had been stored earlier. And one day some men came from Joseph's old country to ask for food. When they approached Joseph, they bowed down to him. Remember the dream?

Joseph recognized them immediately. They were his brothers. After a series of events Joseph finally revealed himself to his brothers and they sobbed together. Then the brothers realized what they had done to Joseph, and what Joseph had become, and they were afraid. They were afraid that he would kill them. But Joseph calmed their fears by making an amazing statement. Hang on to this, friends. Joseph said, "What you intended for evil, God turned for good."

How often, when someone seeks to hurt us or when we feel caught in a nightmare, do we hear people say, "Well, God must have a reason for this." Or, "God, you won't allow me to face more than I can handle. You must think I can handle a lot." In those comments I hear people suggesting that everything that happens to them is what God is trying to do. "Maybe God is trying to teach me a lesson. Maybe God wants to hurt me or punish me for something I've done."

The fact is, friends, that not everything that happens in this world is what God wants. There is evil in this world. Bad things happen to good people. But what the brothers intended for evil, God turned for good.

Romans 8:28 says, "In all things God works for the good of those who love him" (NIV). It doesn't mean that he causes those things. But in all things God can turn something terrible—a nightmare—into a dream come true.

And so, friends, your favorite sports team didn't lose yesterday because God wanted them to lose. Winning and losing in competitive sports is not what the Bible had in mind when a storyteller explains how God is Lord of human history.

When a friend of yours finds out that she has a brain tumor, that's not God trying to hurt that person or teach her a lesson. We live in a broken and frail world. And yet, God can turn that terrible situation into something good.

We see this ultimately through the Cross. Think about it. Jesus came to be loved. He came to be followed. He came to be listened to. What did we do? We killed him. We put him on a cross. Now, from a human point of view, that's the most tragic thing that could ever happen. But God turned that around into something wonderful. He raised Jesus from the dead, and through the Cross and the Resurrection we now have forgiveness. Through this Cross there is power to heal us. Through the Cross and the Resurrection we have eternal life. The most wonderful thing imaginable came from the cruelest tragedy in human history.

If God can reverse death on the Cross, God can remove the barriers that keep us from his guidance. He can turn our nightmares into dreams come true.

A couple in our congregation was living a nightmare. They hit bottom. Their job situation turned sour. Lawsuits and countersuits were filed. It was a terrible mess.

But instead of growing bitter and sour toward God or toward those hurting them, they took a step of faith. They opened their Bible and started to read. And they read like they never read before. They prayed like they never prayed before. And they listened like they never listened before. At one point when they were deciding how to retaliate against those trying to harm them, they read the passage where Jesus says, "Turn the other cheek. Pray for those who persecute you."

So instead of retaliating, they listened to God, who led them to start a new business. Now, I'm happy to say that their new business is thriving. And they are bubbling with joy to see how God has been guiding them through this terrible situation.

Because God loves you so deeply he will guide you. He'll give you his Word as direction. He'll plant dreams in your heart. Maybe you need a dream today. Maybe it's time to slow down and listen, and let God plant dreams in your heart. Maybe you're walking in your dream and it's not going so well. You're wondering, "Lord, where are you?" You can trust today that the Lord is with you. God will never leave you. The Lord will never forsake you. Maybe you feel like you're living in a nightmare. Watch how God is going to turn that nightmare into a dream come true.

Ultimately, when depending on God's love, nothing can defeat us. On God's team we cannot lose. God will guide you. Let's pray together.

This message was preached during a spirited-traditional service by Paul Sorensen, assistant pastor at Community Church of Joy, in Glendale, Arizona.

SPIRITED–TRADITIONAL COMMUNION SERVICE
Sermon Series
Getting to Know the God Who Loves You—
PART TWO

Getting to Know the God of the Second Chance— The Story of Samson

JUDGES 16:23-30

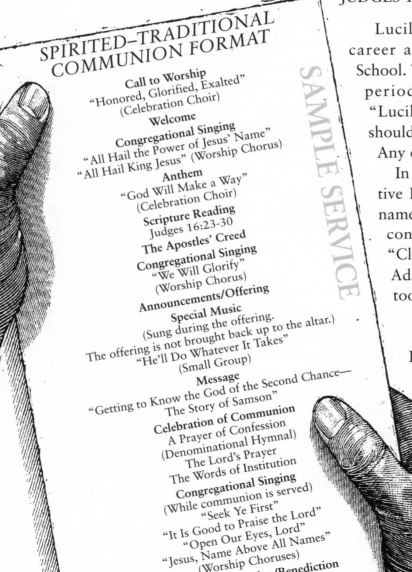

SPIRITED–TRADITIONAL COMMUNION FORMAT

Call to Worship
"Honored, Glorified, Exalted"
(Celebration Choir)

Welcome

Congregational Singing
"All Hail the Power of Jesus' Name"
"All Hail King Jesus" (Worship Chorus)

Anthem
"God Will Make a Way"
(Celebration Choir)

Scripture Reading
Judges 16:23-30

The Apostles' Creed

Congregational Singing
"We Will Glorify"
(Worship Chorus)

Announcements/Offering

Special Music
(Sung during the offering.
The offering is not brought back up to the altar.)
"He'll Do Whatever It Takes"
(Small Group)

Message
"Getting to Know the God of the Second Chance—
The Story of Samson"

Celebration of Communion
A Prayer of Confession
(Denominational Hymnal)
The Lord's Prayer
The Words of Institution

Congregational Singing
(While communion is served)
"Seek Ye First"
"It Is Good to Praise the Lord"
"Open Our Eyes, Lord"
"Jesus, Name Above All Names"
(Worship Choruses)

Communion Blessing/Benediction

SAMPLE SERVICE

Lucille Ball began studying for her acting career at the John Murray-Anderson Drama School. The head teacher, after watching her for a period of time, went to Lucille and said, "Lucille, I've got to tell you something. You should choose any profession other than acting. Any other!"

In 1959, United Universal Picture's Executive Director terminated a young man by the name of Clint Eastwood. When he ended the contract with the would-be actor, he said, "Clint, you have a chip on your tooth, your Adam's apple sticks out too far, and you talk too slow." And Clint was gone.

In 1962, four fearful, knee-shaking musicians auditioned for the first time with Decker Recording. After they played, the executives were clearly not impressed. They said to these four young British men called the Beatles, "We don't like your sound. And by the way, groups with guitars are on the way out!"

And in 1954, the Executive Director of the Grand Ole Opry, after one performance by Elvis, fired him on the spot. He said, "You ain't goin' nowhere son. You ought to go back to drivin' a truck."

All these entertainers went on to be very successful in their careers. They endured the failure. And despite their failure they got a second chance.

If you were to talk to any parent who has raised children into adulthood, any couple who has been married for fifty years or more, or any successful entertainer, you would hear in their conversation at least one word over and over again. The word is *hope*.

Hope. Without it we die. With it we not only survive any challenge but we can even thrive in the midst of adversity. As we continue our series, "Getting to Know the God Who Loves You," we're going to focus on the "God of the Second Chance." We're going to look at how God can give us hope, how God can give us that second opportunity to thrive in the midst of defeat.

In the Bible story about Samson, the people of Israel have lost hope. The oppressors, the Philistines, have pushed them down, abused them, and defeated them. So the Israelites call out to God. And in response, God sends a superhero, Samson. By all accounts, Samson is an extremely muscular, tough, rugged, strong, courageous man.

I know what you're thinking. (Pause) "Much like you, Pastor Paul."

By the way, did you know that after the age of thirty, the average American loses a half a pound of muscle every year? At that rate, I'm due to be out of muscle by next week! Samson I'm not.

Unlike me, Samson was extremely strong. With his own bare hands he tore the gates off the wall of the enemy city. With the jawbone of a donkey he killed a thousand enemy soldiers. With his brute strength he popped open ropes as if they were thread. Samson is Superman, Batman, Ninja Turtles, and Power Rangers all put together in one—at the service of Israel!

But most important, God gives Samson a dream. God puts in Samson's heart the desire to use his strength to help others. To set his people free. To give them a brand new beginning.

Unfortunately, Samson gets diverted, his vision and promise sidetracked. Just as Samson's physical muscles are strong, his moral fiber is weak. Like many superheroes he has a weakness for beautiful women. As the beautiful Delilah seduces him, she draws out of him the secret of his strength.

Before Samson was born, his mother was told by God to never tell the secret of her future son's strength. His hair is the source of his prowess and is never to be cut. In a moment of weakness, Samson reveals that secret to Delilah. While he is sleeping on her lap, she shaves his head.

When Samson awoke his enemies attack. They bind him. And he can't fight back. His strength is gone. They gouge out his eyes and humiliate him by making him a slave.

At the bottom of the pit, at the end of his rope, when he has no hope, God comes to this tragic young man. Samson cries out to the Lord, and the Lord gives him a second chance.

Samson leans against the palace pillars, and with the strength that only God could give, he pushes those pillars apart, collapsing the entire palace and killing thousands of his enemies. Though he died in the rubble, God uses Samson to redeem God's people. God gives them a new hope and a new beginning.

As we ponder this story we might ask, "Why did God put this story in the Bible?" Samson dies with his second chance. It's a story of discouragement. It's a story of hopes gone awry. It's a story of physical strength and moral weakness. But, in reality, what we see in this story is the love and grace of God. Even in Samson's defeat, even in his failure, God brings about a new beginning.

We probably can't relate to Samson's enormous strength. But we can all probably relate to Samson's human character. Like Samson, we've blown it. We've failed miserably. Or maybe someone stood in the way of our goals and plans for life. And now we're living with the resulting pain and brokenness. And at the end of this episode perhaps we've lost our hope. But God, in his goodness, now and throughout your life, gives you a second chance, just as God did for Samson; a new beginning; a fresh opportunity to try again.

God gives you a second chance in three specific ways.

First, God gives you a second chance by breaking your bondages.

I've got some plastic "rope" used by police officers. If I could have a helper here tie my hands . . . Real tight . . . Thanks. Now, do you think I can break this? It's pretty tight. In the back you can hardly see these ropes binding my hands. So often in our lives there are things that bind us that no one else can see.

A person in bondage came to me for help. He said, "Pastor, several years ago my life went on a trajectory of destruction. It was a bad habit that hurt me, my family, and almost destroyed me. I felt like someone placed handcuffs on my wrists. And no matter how hard I pulled and strove to break those handcuffs, I couldn't. I was locked in chains."

As we talked together and prayed over time, the power of God, the power that moved that stone from the tomb, the same power of Jesus Christ, began to cut through his handcuffs. My friend shared his weakness and struggles honestly. And through God's power, those chains began to break.

Our God is in the chain-breaking business. What we cannot defeat by ourselves—our failures and weaknesses—God can. God breaks our bonds.

And so now, (to the helper up front) . . . Will you cut these bondages off? You did remember to bring the scissors I asked you to bring, didn't you? You do have the scissors? Thanks.

God breaks our bondages just as _____ broke mine. God has the power that we don't have to break our chains. But when we cry out, "Lord, help," God will respond.

Second, God gives you a second chance by healing your hurts.

Have you ever had your head shaved? Not literally, like Charles Barclay, Michael Jordan, or Samson. Rather, have you ever had a dream, and then someone came and took it right off the top of your head? Some circumstance defeated you? Or maybe you made a bad decision that rubbed others wrongly and that robbed you of an opportunity? It was like the power of your dream was drained from your body? You couldn't see the future? You felt hopeless, discouraged, depressed?

And as that happened to you, the hurt came. And hurt, if it lingers for a time, can turn to bitterness. And that bitterness can paralyze you—keeping you from moving forward with your life.

The good news is that Jesus Christ comes to move though the corridors of your heart to heal your hurt. He'll give you the strength to forgive and to let go, to bring balm and salve to those areas of pain. Jesus Christ heals your pain.

Third, God gives you a second chance by focusing your future.

When Florence Chadwick looked before her all she saw was a wall of fog. Her body was numb. She had been swimming for over sixteen hours. Florence Chadwick had already broken the world record by being the first woman to swim the English Channel back and forth. Now she was facing the challenge of swimming from Catalina Island to the California coast.

On that 4th of July, 1952, as Florence swam, the sea felt like an ice bath. The fog was so thick that she could hardly see her support boat. Sharks moved toward her and only the rifle fire kept them away. The fierce cold sea tried to hold her back. But she swam on hour after hour. Millions of people watched her on national television.

Her mother and her trainer tried to encourage her from the support boat. They said, "Florence, you're almost there." But all she could see was the fog. They said, "Florence, don't give up." She had never given up before. But in that moment of pain, with the fog all around her, she said, "Lift me into the boat."

When she was finally onboard, she discovered that she was only one-half mile from the shore.

Hours later, as she was still thawing out from the cold, she told a reporter, "I don't mean to make excuses for myself, but if I only could have seen the shore, I think I would have made it."

It wasn't the cold that defeated her. It wasn't the fatigue that did her in. It was the fog. She had lost sight of her goal.

Two months later Florence tried it again. This time with faith firmly fixed in her heart. This time with a clear picture of the goal. Even though the fog this second time was just as dense, she saw in her mind the picture of the shore beyond the fog. She knew it was there. She swam hard and she made it.

Florence was the first woman ever to swim the Catalina Channel. And she defeated the men's record by two hours in the process.

Sometimes we get discouraged. It's as though we're in a fog. Our hurts, failures, and frustrations keep us from seeing ahead. But Jesus Christ comes to give us a picture of the future. A vision of what we cannot see in the midst of our pain.

God did it for Samson. God does it for us. God shows us that failure is never final. That a second chance is possible. That even death is not the end. Even if we face death, God has an eternal future that is beautiful and wonderful.

Perhaps you feel like you're in a fog right now. God comes to you to give you a positive picture of the future. It may seem like an end, but instead it is an opportunity for a new beginning. It's a picture of hope.

The story of Samson reminds us that God heals our hurts. God breaks our bondages. God focuses our future and gives us a second chance.

But there's another reason why the Bible preserves the story of Samson. It isn't just for us.

All around us there are people who need a second chance. People in your neighborhood. Friends at work. Their family has given up on them. Their friends have given up on them. Their church has given up on them. And some of them have even given up on themselves. So what can we do?

We can tell them this good news. We can tell them that our God is a God of the second chance. That our God forgives and heals. That God breaks the bonds. Let's do that! Let's tell them! Let's tell them the story of Jesus and the God of the second chance!

This message was preached during a spirited-traditional service by Paul Sorensen, assistant pastor at Community Church of Joy in Glendale, Arizona.

Spirited-Traditional Choral Resources

"And the Father Will Dance"
Words and Music: Mark Hayes
Arrangement: Mark Hayes
Copyright © 1983 Hinshaw Music, Inc.

"Be the One"
Words and Music: Don Koch, Al Denson, Dave Clark
Arrangement: John E. Coates
Copyright © 1990 Paragon Music Corp.

"Before the Rocks Cry Out"
Words and Music: Tim Sheppard
Arrangement: Tammy Waldrop, Bruce Greer
Copyright © 1987, 1990 Tim Sheppard Music

"Call on Him"
Words and Music: John Leavitt
Arrangement: Hal Leonard
Copyright © 1992 Hal Leonard Publishing Corp.

"Come and Worship"
Words and Music: Don Moen
Arrangement: Mark Hayes
Copyright © 1988 Integrity's Hosanna! Music

"Come, Let Us Sing for Joy"
Words and Music: John E. Coates
Arrangement: Don Hart
Copyright © 1995 Word Music

"Candlelight Carol"
Words and Music: John Rutter
Arrangement: John Rutter
Copyright © 1985 Oxford University Press

"Creation Praise!"
Words and Music: Benjamin Harlan, J. Paul Williams
Arrangement: Benjamin Harlan
Copyright © 1990 GlorySound

"Delight in the Lord"
Words and Music: Bruce Greer, Psalm 37
Arrangement: Bruce Greer
Copyright © 1990 Word Music

"Gloria"
(from *The Kingdom Song*)
Words and Music: Mark Hayes
Arrangement: Mark Hayes
Copyright © 1990 Birdwing Music

"Gloria"
(from The Sounds of Christmas series)
Words and Music: Antonio Vivaldi
Arrangement: Stan Pethel
Copyright © 1994 New Spring Publishing

"God Will Make a Way"
Words and Music: Don Moen
Arrangement: Camp Kirkland, Tom Fettke
Copyright © 1990/1992 Integrity's Hosanna! Music

"Grace Upon Grace"
Words and Music: Stan Pethel
Arrangement: Stan Pethel
Copyright © 1994 New Spring Publishing

"Holy Is He (Holy, Holy, Holy)"

Words and Music: David T. Clydesdale, Claire
   Cloninger
Arrangement: David T. Clydesdale
Copyright © 1985 Royal Tapestry Music

"Honored, Glorified, Exalted"

Words and Music: Randy Vader, Jay Rouse
Arrangement: Camp Kirkland
Copyright © 1989 Gaither Music Company

"I See the Lord"

Words and Music: John Chisum, Don Moen
Arrangement: Dan Burgess
Copyright © 1994 Integrity's Hosanna! Music

"Jesus Is Alive"

Words and Music: Ron Kenoly
Arrangement: Dan Burgess
Copyright © 1987 Integrity's Hosanna! Music

"Jesus, Keep Me Near the Cross"

Words and Music: Fanny J. Crosby, William H.
   Doane
Arrangement: Robert Sterling
Copyright © 1984 GlorySound

"Jesus, the One and Only"

Words and Music: Babbie Mason
Arrangement: Ken Barker
Copyright © 1988, 1989 Word Music

"No Stone"

Words and Music: Lowell Alexander, Steve
   Amerson
Arrangement: Gary Rhodes
Copyright © 1992 Birdwing Music

"O Lord, I Will Praise You" (medley)

Words and Music: Gloria Gaither, Michael W.
   Smith/Jean Sibelius, Phill McHugh, Tom Fettke
Arrangement: Tom Fettke
Copyright © 1988 Gaither Music Co./© 1988
   River Oaks Music Co./Word Music

"Sing Out a Song!"

Words and Music: Nancy Price, Don Besig
Arrangement: Larry Mayfield
Copyright © 1989 GlorySound

"Sing Unto the Lord"

Words and Music: Charles Yannerella
Arrangement: Charles Yannerella
Copyright © 1983 Breckenhorst Press, Inc.

"Sound His Praise"

Words and Music: Melody Tunney
Arrangement: Joseph Linn
Copyright © 1983 Laurel Press

"Starlight"

Words and Music: R. Kelso Carter/Spiritual/
   Edward Mote, William B. Bradbury
Arrangement: Dave Williamson
Copyright © 1991 New Spring Publishing/© 1991
   New Spring Publishing

"Swing Low/Swing Down"

Words and Music: Keith Thomas, Traditional
   Spirituals
Arrangement: Tom Fettke
Copyright © 1981, 1994 Word Music

"The Majesty and Glory of Your Name"

Words and Music: Tom Fettke, Linda Lee Johnson
Arrangement: Don Hart
Copyright © 1986, 1990 Meadowgreen Music Co.

"Then Will the Very Rocks Cry Out"

Words and Music: Gary McSpadden, Bill George, John W. Thompson, Randy L. Scruggs
Arrangement: Tom Fettke
Copyright © 1979 Norman Clayton Publishing Co.

"There Is Peace"

Words and Music: Dick and Melodie Tunney
Arrangement: Mark Hayes
Copyright © 1984, 1985 Kaanapali Music

"Worthy, Faithful and Righteous"

Words and Music: Claire Cloninger, Don Koch
Arrangement: Dan Burgess
Copyright © 1989, 1991 Integrity's Hosanna! Music/© 1986 Integrity's Hosanna! Music

"Worthy Melody (Worthy You Are Worthy/Jesus You Are Worthy)"

Words and Music: Don Moen/Don Moen
Arrangement: Bill Wolaver
Copyright © 1990, 1991 BMG Songs, Inc.

Part 3

CONTEMPORARY PRAISE SERVICES

*Contemporary Praise Services use contemporary music
to lead believers into worship.
These services emphasize congregational participation.
While geared to believers,
these services take seriously the needs of guests
and nonchurchgoing people.
Contemporary Praise Services are therefore
believer-oriented,
but visitor-friendly.*

Selecting Songs and Choruses for a Contemporary Worship Service

CATHY TOWNLEY

During four years of leading and planning contemporary worship in a well-established church, I learned a lot about selecting music. The music marketplace is loaded with many contemporary Christian songs—almost too many. A worship leader can feel overwhelmed sometimes when trying to wade through the copious quantities of material to find the right songs for a particular setting. I've found that it simplifies the process a little by thinking through how we choose music. Here's a few ideas that may help:

1. Keep it simple. Some of the best songs are short, simple, and repetitive. Known as "praise choruses," these songs may at first seem "simplistic" to an accomplished musician. More often than not, however, the simple, repetitive tunes create a profound worship experience for people. Repetition is a well-known contemplative act that serves to clear the mind and center the person in praise of the Lord. Frequently, praise choruses center on a Bible verse that has been adapted to fit a melody. Because they're short, choruses are easy to learn and remember, and usually easy to sing. Repetition offers the worshiper a chance to meditate on the message expressed in the chorus.

2. Welcome newcomers. When choosing contemporary music I tend to think first in terms of newcomers. How will people feel if they are at our worship service for the first time? How about those who may never have been to a church at all (or at least not for a very long time)? Will they be able to relate to the worship service? Will they be able to participate in some way? Songs that invite newcomer participation will either be easy to learn or will have a refrain that people can easily sing. Repeating simple songs or refrains of solos helps newcomers catch on so that they can sing along. Another kind of newcomer-oriented music is the performance song. Well-done and well-placed performance songs by a contemporary vocal team can establish a moving environment for worship.

3. Network. I find most of our "outside" music through networking. We write a lot of our own music, but we do use a significant amount of music currently on the market. Ask the members of your worship leadership team (vocal team), or ask your congregation what they like. I get many fresh ideas from the people who attend our contemporary service or who help lead it. I also get ideas from other churches. I try to find out what my colleagues use in worship. When I can, I visit other congregations that offer contemporary worship and I take back the songs I think will suit our worship style.

4. Discover your worship style. Worship can take on many different forms. At least three of the commonly understood models are: praise and worship, liturgical, and blended. Effective praise and worship or blended models—services that use a block of three to five worship choruses in a row—utilize songs that go together. If you use the liturgical model, you will want to use songs that relate to the various parts of the worship experience. For example, you'll need songs for the gathering, the invitation to worship, praise, prayer, offering, Scripture, a sermon response, communion, possibly healing (for a service in which there is anointing with oil), and a dismissal. Most worship songbooks offer a cross-reference index of themes.

5. Think thematically. Some worship leaders plan the whole service based around a single theme. Everything in the entire service relates to that theme. Therefore, you need to find songs to suit the theme of the day. Most contemporary Christian music books make this easy to do because they typically cross-reference according to theme and sometimes to scripture reference.

6. Integrate styles. I love upbeat songs. I like rock, gospel, jazz, and anything that has a lot of rhythm. I love to sing those songs and clap my hands, allowing me to get into the worship experience with my whole soul. However, everyone is different. People will be reached in different ways through different styles. Many appreciate a flow of music,

which goes from upbeat to slow and meditative, and then perhaps back to something a little upbeat again. Also, globalization has ushered in an ethnic movement in pop music—African, Latin, calypso, reggae, Native American. People expect that worship will affect their bodies. They want to be moved into praise. Blending styles in the same service will help to do that.

7. Discover personal favorites. Even though I usually think of the newcomer first, I also like to pick songs for my own benefit as well. As a worship leader, you need not prefer everything that you sing. Other people may like music you don't, or there may be other reasons to choose certain songs. However, you will be a music barometer for part of your congregation. And you'll do a good job of leading what you like. To find music and artists you personally enjoy, you may want to listen to the radio. Many communities have at least one contemporary Christian music station. Some have more than one. Listen to them all, because they're probably different. You'll get to know the popular artists, and you'll discover who you like. You'll hear music that will engage your spirit, music you will want to use in your worship services. Some songs will be geared for performance and others will be songs that your congregation can sing. If you don't have a contemporary Christian music station, check out your local Christian bookstore. Many of them allow you to preview tapes and CDs before you decide to make a purchase. Spend some hours getting introduced to the latest in contemporary Christian music and praise songs.

8. Honor God's diversity. In my denominational home (United Methodist) we expressly value diversity. We represent many layers in the theological spectrum. I prefer to use music that offers a variety of images of God. The use of diverse images of God is welcoming to newcomers. When worship is open to newcomers, we presume that each person is different, and that the Holy Spirit will use different languages to communicate the gospel to different people. For example, in much of contemporary Christian music, God is portrayed as "Warrior" and "the Almighty." In our music we think it's also important to sing about the God who is the Suffering Servant, or as the One who nurtures. When we can, we utilize "inclusive language" in addition to songs about God who is Father.

9. Include traditional hymns. Some people in your congregation will want to hear and sing hymns with which they were raised. We often include traditional hymns along with our contemporary music. Typically, we write a chord chart for the hymns and then transpose the key into one that is more singable (usually lower). Playing a traditional hymn from a chord chart in and of itself usually changes the way the hymn sounds. Add a slightly different rhythm or style to the hymn, or change some of the harmonics, and you have a brand new song. (See Part 2: Spirited-Traditional Worship.)

10. Write your own music. Personal creativity is a must, I believe, for churches changing to contemporary worship. We expect this kind of imagination from a message by the pastor. So what could be more contemporary than an original musical composition for a specific place and time? Writing our own music promotes creativity, commitment, fun, involvement, and spiritual growth. Our music has improved tremendously since the beginning, and yours probably will, too. And if your music is good, and you are ready for it, offer it to other churches. I'm always on the lookout for new music from other congregations. It sounds different from our music, and it's usually different from the music found in bookstores or heard on the radio. Don't be shy. Accept God's challenge to express your spiritual journey and your musical gifts in this way.

Cathy Townley is currently worship director of Crossroads, a new United Methodist church in Lakeville, Minnesota. She is also president of Wellsprings Unlimited, which provides contemporary worship music and workshops for churches. She has published *Deeper Well Music,* volumes 1 and 2, through Wellsprings Unlimited, which features worship music from the contemporary service at her church. She has also coauthored *Come Celebrate! A Guide to Planning Contemporary Worship* (Abingdon Press, 1995) and compiled a collection of ninety songs called *Come Celebrate! The Songbook* (Abingdon Press, 1995).

Managing the Flow of Worship

CRAIG KENNET MILLER

What would it be like to be a member of the congregation in a worship service that you designed? There is a remarkable difference between leading the worship and experiencing the worship. Those of us who are used to leading the worship think everyone out there is moving through the service the same way we are. But this is not generally the case. There is a big difference between preaching a sermon and listening to it, between singing in the choir and

hearing it, and between praying a prayer and listening to it.

The first step toward making your praise worship service an engaging and life-changing experience is to imagine you are in the congregation so you can see if the service has flow and movement. Flow has to do with the sense of energy and natural unfolding of the service of worship, like a stream flowing as opposed to an assortment of unconnected parts. Movement has to do with a destination for the service, like a train bound for a delivery point.

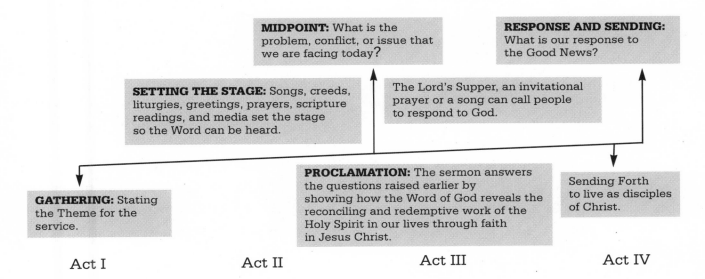

MIDPOINT: What is the problem, conflict, or issue that we are facing today?

RESPONSE AND SENDING: What is our response to the Good News?

SETTING THE STAGE: Songs, creeds, liturgies, greetings, prayers, scripture readings, and media set the stage so the Word can be heard.

The Lord's Supper, an invitational prayer or a song can call people to respond to God.

GATHERING: Stating the Theme for the service.

PROCLAMATION: The sermon answers the questions raised earlier by showing how the Word of God reveals the reconciling and redemptive work of the Holy Spirit in our lives through faith in Jesus Christ.

Sending Forth to live as disciples of Christ.

Act I   Act II   Act III   Act IV

As the director of the divine drama of worship your mission is to create an experience of worship that unfolds from Act I to Act IV in a way that moves people to a greater awareness of the grace of God as found through faith in Jesus Christ. Your goal is to challenge people to make some kind of decision as to how they are going to live differently because of what God has called them to be. One way to envision a contemporary praise service is to look at the following diagram:

Act I: The Gathering

The gathering may start with a call to worship, a hymn, an anthem by the choir or a song by a soloist, a video clip or a dramatic sketch. Whatever the elements used, vital to the flow of worship is laying out the theme for the service. In a great movie the first scene sets the tone, the setting, and the mood for the whole work. The first scene of your service raises the expectation of what this service is about and who it is for.

For example, if the service starts out with ten minutes of announcements informing the congregation of various meetings and events, then everyone knows that the service is for the insiders—those who are members of the church. Often I have heard someone say at the beginning of the service, "A potluck dinner will be held at Nate and Millie's house. Everyone is invited." As a visitor I immediately feel shut out because I don't know Nate and Millie, and I certainly don't know where they live.

On the other hand, if the service starts out with a brief prayer and a series of uplifting songs then I know we have all come to worship God. Or if it starts out with a dramatic sketch or a riveting video or a thought provoking song that introduces a relevant theme

for the service, then I am onboard immediately because I want to know what is going to happen next.

Act II: Setting the Stage

The careful worship producer will set the stage by introducing various elements of worship that build momentum. Prayers, creeds, liturgies, songs, scripture readings, anthems, solos, multimedia, and greetings are all elements that can help set the mood for a readiness to hear the gospel. The careful planner chooses those elements that best enhance the congregation's ability to interact with the Word.

Act III: Proclamation

At the midpoint of a movie you are immersed in the conflict, the problem, or the dilemma that the main character of the story is facing. There is creative tension because you do not know how it is going to turn out. You are ready for something to help make sense out of the chaos and the conflict. The key to vital contemporary worship is to be able to offer a message that speaks to the real needs and concerns of the congregation. Few souls are going to be touched if the preacher focuses only on general ideas about theology or human experience. People deserve to hear a message of hope that speaks directly to their lives.

The pivotal issue of the service can be raised by the first line of the sermon, by a song, by a video clip, or a dramatic sketch. If the theme is reconciling family differences, perhaps you would introduce a video clip from the movie *Reality Bites,* which shows a young woman struggling with how to talk to her divorced parents. Maybe you could do a dramatic sketch centered around the dinner table with Dad waiting for everyone to get home so he can serve dinner to them. His question might be, "Where has my family gone?" The message that follows might focus on how God brought Joseph's family back to him and how Joseph was able to forgive his brothers.

Act IV: Response and Sending Out

At the conclusion of the message you will want to offer people an opportunity to respond to the message they have heard. People may be invited to take part in the Lord's Supper, sing a song, or consider their relationship with God in prayer.

The service ends by sending people forth into the world to live as Christian disciples. The key to the end of the service is to offer some word of hope and some way of taking the gospel with them as they head back into the world.

The challenge for the worship leader is to put himself or herself in the shoes of the participants and to experience the service from their perspective. The joy is found in creating a flow of worship that brings people to a place where they can affirm their faith in God and see their situations and their lives from God's perspective. Each element of the service plays an integral part in moving people toward a response to God's call that day. The careful planner is willing to cut out anything that is not necessary for that day and to add only that which enhances the ability for the Word to be heard.

Dr. Craig Kennet Miller is the coauthor of *Contemporary Worship for the 21st Century: Worship or Evangelism?* (Discipleship Resources, 1994). He has also written *Baby Boomer Spirituality: Ten Essential Values of a Generation.* He is the director of New Congregational Development for the General Board of Discipleship of The United Methodist Church based in Nashville. He has also served as an adjunct professor at Fuller Theological Seminary.

Leading Contemporary Worship

TIM AND JAN WRIGHT

Many contemporary praise services build on one or more "worship packages," a series of worship choruses/hymns sung back to back. Leading these worship segments in a way that invites participation on the part of newcomers requires a different mind-set than for those already committed to Christian worship. The following guidelines can provide a starting point as you seek to make your time of worship more dynamic and inclusive:

1. Plan worship. The main job of the worship leader is to ensure an excellent flow to the worship service. To make that happen, effective worship leaders do most of their work before the service by carefully planning the worship experience. Many worship leaders, regrettably, use the "move with the mood" approach to worship. They choose a few worship choruses for the service but other than that, the shaping of the worship experience takes place during the service. For instance, the number of times the songs are sung is dependent on the "feel" on the stage or in the congregation. Some worship choruses are sung over and over again because the worship leader feels inspired to do so. Certainly as worship leaders we want to be sensitive to the working of the Spirit. The Spirit should be free to do what God wants in worship. At times we may sense that God is using a particular chorus to touch the hearts of the worshipers, so it bears repeating. However, when planning a service that invites and draws in newcomers, a more carefully defined worship package may prove more effective. Newcomers are being introduced to such an experience perhaps for the first time. They may not understand the subtle atmospheric nuances that are felt by the worship leader or committed Christians. They may find the "lack of planning" or the monotonous repetition of a chorus frustrating and even irritating.

A better approach to worship calls for the worship leader and primary accompanist to plan the worship package(s). The best preachers don't wing it on Sunday. They pray over the text, study it, pray some more, write the message or an outline, learn it, and then present it. The most effective messages grow out of careful, prayerful planning. The same holds true for worship. Outreached-focused worship leaders and their teams carefully choose worship choruses that have a flow to them. For example, starting with a few up-tempo songs and moving into more contemplative, worshipful songs can make for a very dynamic package. Planning also includes knowing exactly how many times each song will be sung, when the key will change, when people will be invited to stand or sit (and don't stand too long!), and how the transition will take place into the next song. Instead of detracting from the spontaneity of the Spirit, such attention to detail can actually enhance the worship climate. Prayerful planning gives a sense of continuity and excellence to the worship package. The leader may, at times, feel a need to repeat a chorus beyond what was planned for. But being well prepared for the worship set makes for a smoother, more worshipful experience.

2. Know the mood you want to set. In developing the worship package for any given Sunday, give careful consideration to the climate of the worship that choruses will set. Do you want an up-tempo package of choruses that energizes people? Or do you want to create a contemplative, worshipful mood? Our hunch is that guests prefer a more upbeat service. Lengthy periods of contemplative worship encourage people to focus on worshiping God, which can come across as too "religious" for guests. They will feel excluded because they may not be

sure they believe in God, let alone feel moved to worship him. As mentioned above, an appropriate balance of high energy songs and contemplative choruses may be the best option.

3. Limit worship. Exciting, dynamic, excellent worship can be very effective in demonstrating the joy and hope of the gospel to newcomers. However, too much of a good thing can wear them out. While believers may enjoy a thirty- to forty-minute worship set, guests and first-time worshipers will find it wearying—because they don't know the songs or don't have a full appreciation for worship.

While in France I (Tim) sat through four contemporary praise services in one day. While I deeply appreciated the passion for worship that I experienced, I was absolutely worn out. Not from participating, but from my inability to communicate with the culture of worship. Because the words were in French, I couldn't sing along. I was an outsider looking in. Ten to twenty minutes may have been O.K. But forty minutes of worship choruses in French, four times, was too much.

Even when the words are in the language of the guest, too much worship will drain a newcomer rather than inspire and encourage him or her to focus on God. Find other times for extended periods of worship for believers if you want to attract and hold newcomers on Sunday morning. Fifteen to twenty minutes of contemporary praise worship is long enough for them. Ten to fifteen minutes may even be better.

4. Use culturally relevant styles of music. Use the kinds of music your target audience listens to on the radio. If the top music stations in your area feature pop/adult contemporary music, find choruses that capture that flavor. If your audience prefers country music, use country-flavored Christian worship songs. Southern Gospel music, in a pop-oriented culture, will set a climate your audience will not appreciate. Pop music in a country-oriented town will not likely appeal to that audience. While variety works occasionally, keep your musical styles consistent and in line with the music of your culture.

5. Rehearse the worship package. Excellence in leading the worship set is as important as excellence in presentational music. To make the set effective the band and singers will want to rehearse it as if they were leading worship on Sunday. This gives everyone a chance to know when a chorus will be repeated, when the transitions will occur, and so on.

The goal is to get everyone on the same page. A confident worship team makes for a more relaxed, enjoyable worship service.

6. Develop a simple communication system. As previously mentioned, there will be occasions when the worship plan changes—right on the platform! If the leader senses the need to cut a song short, eliminate a song, or repeat a song, he or she needs a way to communicate that to the worship team. Stopping the service to make a change, or yelling the change to the team during worship won't cut it. The worship leader needs to develop a set of communication signals that the

entire team understands. For example, perhaps the leader wants to repeat a chorus, so she very subtly twirls her hand indicating her desire to sing the song again. Maybe the leader wants to cut the song short so he holds up a closed fist to alert the band and

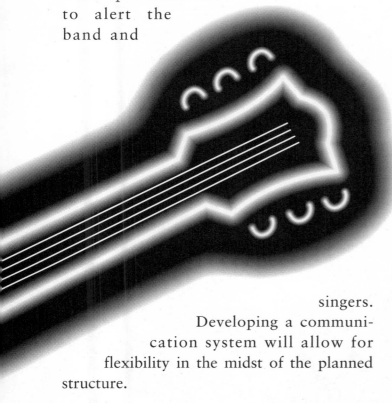

singers. Developing a communication system will allow for flexibility in the midst of the planned structure.

7. Invite participation, don't demand it. Newcomers always respond best to loving invitations. Confrontation turns them off. Invitational worship simply and gently encourages people to participate in the worship experience if they so desire. It says, "We're going to worship together this morning. If you like to sing, this is your chance. If you enjoy listening to great music, feel free to sit back and do just that." Not everybody likes to sing, or can sing. And, again, newcomers will not know the songs. Giving people the option to listen rather than sing puts the nonparticipants at ease.

8. Let the music draw people into worship. The most compelling worship leaders say very little. They may invite people to sing and worship at the beginning of the worship set. They may also take a moment between songs to ask the audience to stand or sit. But the fewer words spoken, the better. Phrases like, "You can do better than that!" or "Let's sing with more energy!" or "Let's all raise our hands together on this song," force people, especially guests, to do things that they may not want to do. Dynamic worship leaders carefully plan out the choices of choruses and allow those songs to create a mood. They let the songs move people to respond in the way individuals feel most comfortable. If someone raises his or her hands, great. Not everyone has to do the same to worship. Not everyone feels like singing with energy, or even singing at all. Let the Spirit, through the music, move people to respond.

9. Evaluate the worship segment. After the service, ask yourself, "Did the worship package create the mood we had hoped for? Did the songs flow together nicely or did the transitions feel choppy? Was the set too uptempo? Too slow? Just right? Did people seem to be participating? Did we use too many new songs? Was the worship team prepared? Did we as a team stay alert to what was happening on stage and in the audience? What can we do better?"

You may want to talk to a few worshipers to get their read on the worship segment. If possible, try to find out how first-time guests, particularly those new to any kind of worship experience, are responding to the service and the time of worship.

Developing a Praise Band

RICHARD A. LESLIE

When the psalmist wrote Psalm 150, naming the instruments of praise for his day, he certainly had no idea what was to come. For obvious reasons he did not include electric guitars, digital drums, and pipe organs with MIDI interface and built-in synthesizers. But the psalmist did include the instruments of praise for his time: trumpets, harps, lyres, tambourines, strings, flutes, and cymbals. That assembly sounds like a very decent praise band in itself. So if you're ready to develop a group of instrumentalists to help lead worship, you have permission from the psalmist. Below are some practical ideas on how to get started.

A basic contemporary band consists of a rhythm section, with one of the instruments being capable of playing the melody line. You can start with a piano, electric or acoustic bass, and drums. The piano can play the chord patterns as well as a melody line. The bass and drums are your basic rhythm section. Next, you can add an acoustic guitar to take over the chords, allowing the piano to add the "ruffles and flourishes." The guitar can trade off the melody line with the piano at times, especially on the softer parts.

Once the rhythm section is set, other melody instruments such as the flute, trumpet, or saxophone can be added. Any good player can take a melody part and embellish it or take a solo line for variety. As your program expands and you find more and more talent for your band, add an entire brass section, woodwinds, a saxophone section, strings, and more percussion. Again, start with the basics and grow from there.

You may choose to use professional players for your basic four: keyboard, bass, drums, and lead melody player. This will ensure quality of sound to which you can add amateur players from your congregation. I have, however, heard excellent praise bands made up of committed members who love their Lord and love to lead people in worship. Their commitment to the cause is more important than their expertise as musicians.

A number of publishers provide music for praise bands. You can find music for almost any level of playing skill from basic simplified arrangements of praise songs to the most demanding charts for professional players. Check out Integrity's Hosanna! as well as Word, The Vineyard, Maranatha! and Lillenas. More music for praise bands is being published each week.

One very important point to remember: Ask your players for a strong commitment to the band. Make it a small group ministry by setting the expectations clearly, studying scripture together, praying together, and affirming their efforts every chance you get. Your band must see themselves as part of a ministry team that is being used by God for the cause of the gospel of Jesus Christ, which is one more reason for using committed team members rather than hired professionals.

I ask interested players to meet with me to discuss expectations; to hear their musical "history," to hear them play, and then to invite them to sit in on a rehearsal. I check for "prima donnas" and potential spiritual red flags. Remember, your church probably does not ask someone who cannot teach to instruct the new member class. You have a responsibility to graciously discourage anyone who would be a real detriment to your worship band. Usually, when a member who should not be playing hears the expectations—both musical and spiritual—she or he will take herself or himself out of consideration. If that happens, be sure to work with other staff members to find that person a place to serve that is appropriate to her or his gifts and talents.

Tapes and MIDIs

If the talent is not there, or your church is small, there are alternatives to a live band. Accompaniment tapes are available with many praise songs and medleys of praise songs. These usually come in a split-track format, meaning you can add the voices into the sound system or just use the instrumental accompaniment. Tapes are a great way to start. Your band can play along. (That can, however, produce some potentially disastrous results if the band doesn't stay with the tape.)

Another alternative comes from the use of General MIDI keyboards with published or home produced diskettes. *MIDI* stands for "Musical Instrument Digital Interface." That simply means that keyboard and computers and other MIDI instruments can "talk" to each other and play together. The new organ at Salem Lutheran Church in Tomball, Texas, for example, will allow for the pipe organ, several keyboards, lights, sound, and video to be linked and coordinated. New technologies now allow church musicians tremendous possibilities. (I personally think that Bach would have been electrified by the potential!)

Again, Integrity's Hosanna!, as well as other vendors, produce General MIDI diskettes of their music. These diskettes are compatible with any keyboard that uses the General MIDI format. They contain what are known as sequences. These are not recordings but digital information allowing your keyboard to play the music included on the diskette. The advantage over tapes is that with the digital input the tempos can be changed without changing the pitch. The arrangement can also be transposed to a higher or lower key, and any live instrument can be added to or deleted from the keyboard. In other words, if your drummer calls in sick at the last moment, you can include the drum part from the disk. Or, if you have a keyboard player, drums, and bass, you can delete those parts from the disk and the instrumentalists can play live. The quality of a full blown band is there on the MIDI disk, but the possibility of using any and all live musicians still exists. Also, if your trumpet player can handle only a second or third part, the disk can play the full brass section while your trumpet player joins in as he or she can.

I use a Korg 14 interactive workstation as my basic keyboard. It allows me to produce my own sequences and arrangements quickly and easily, or I can use the published disks. Korg, Roland, Yamaha, Ensonic, and many other fine companies are producing new instruments to make all this easier to do. (Be sure, when purchasing a new keyboard, to look for the General MIDI logo.)

For your more traditional needs, General MIDI diskettes are being produced with full symphony orchestra accompaniments of hymns. The organist can play along, making for some wonderful sounds and exciting worship experiences. Check out a California company called Worship Solutions.

Martin Luther believed that every form of art and music should be employed for the sake of the gospel. He also used the latest technology of his day—the printing press—to further the Kingdom. What a great day of opportunity we live in: The message of Christ's love and forgiveness can be flashed around the world to millions of computers on the Internet. The most culturally relevant music, drama, art, communications skills, and technologies now make the power of the gospel available as never before. We can certainly join with the psalmist in using every instrument of praise available to us to lift the name of Jesus before a hurting and dying world.

Richard A. Leslie is the minister of music at Salem Lutheran Church in Tomball, Texas.

Tips for Finding and Recruiting Musicians

TIM WRIGHT

Finding and recruiting musicians poses perhaps the biggest challenge in implementing a contemporary service. Because most established congregations tend to offer only traditional forms of worship, they have not done well in attracting or keeping contemporary musicians.

However, many communities have contemporary musicians who long to use their talents for the Lord. They often haven't found a church that validates their gifts and musical preferences. Once a congregation gains a reputation for using contemporary music, the musicians tend to come out of the woodwork.

The following tips may help you as you look for and recruit contemporary musicians:

1. Pray for musicians. If God has truly called your church to create a contemporary worship service, then ask God to send you the musicians. Those of us who help congregations implement new styles of worship have heard stories of how once a church made the decision to offer an alternative ser-

vice, the musicians "suddenly appeared." Invite God to lead you to the right people and the right people to you.

2. Determine your needs. What instruments are you looking for? Drums? Bass guitar? Keyboards? How many vocalists do you envision in the praise team? What kinds of voices? Tenors? Altos? All men? A mixed group of men and women? Contemporary praise music typically does not use four-part harmony. Four-part harmony gives the music more of a country or Southern Gospel sound. But the Southern Gospel quartet music of the mid-twentieth century, which accompanied itinerant revival buses, is unlikely to attract newcomers to your contemporary praise worship service. Furthermore, too many voices gives the music a choral sound rather than a contemporary pop sound that puts the newcomer at ease.

3. Advertise in your congregation. Let your people know about the new service and the need for musicians. You might find some surprises—people with gifts and talents whom you never knew existed. Or it may be that a member of your church knows someone who would enjoy the chance to be a part of the new band.

4. Advertise on the radio. Many communities now have radio stations playing contemporary Christian music. Buying ads that specifically share what musicians you are looking for may help you find and reach some "unconnected" singers and instrumentalists. Most Christians, however, don't listen to any kind of Christian radio. So you may want to find a "secular" station that plays music stylistically close to what you hope to offer in your services and buy some ads with them. This will cost money, and advertising on radio may or may not get you what you need, so be very clear and specific in the ad.

We've tried radio a few times with mixed results. One time we had several responses to the ads and wound up with a few new band members. Another time we came up with zero help. No interest and no new musicians. Make sure you count the cost before you advertise.

5. Use a local Christian bookstore. Many Christian bookstores carry a wide variety of CDs and tapes featuring contemporary Christian artists. These stores also sell "vocal accompaniment tracks"—tapes with full orchestration but no voices. Singers use these when they don't have a band available to them. Posting "musicians wanted" posters in these areas of the bookstore may net you a few good recruits. Ask your local Christian bookstore if they might be willing to let you put posters up for a few weeks.

6. Use local newspapers. Taking out ads in neighborhood newspapers may also help you find some new musicians. Some communities have newspapers or newsletters geared to musicians. These might help you better target your message.

7. Look for an existing group. There may be a local Christian group already formed in your community. Their ministry consists of local and regional concerts. But they may jump at the chance to "perform" every weekend at your church.

A more daring approach is one used by our senior pastor when he was a youth director in Minneapolis. He needed a band for a new contemporary service. So he invited a local band of high

school students to lead the service. They were eager to play as much as possible. This was not a Christian group, however. Nor were most of the musicians Christians. But under the pastor's direction they found Christian music, and in the process many of them met Jesus as Lord.

At our congregation, we insist that our upfront worship leaders have a relationship with Jesus. Since they lead worship and invite people to consider Jesus through their singing, knowing the purpose of their music is vitally important. However, we have used instrumentalists who weren't believers, and many of them became believers as a result of their contact with the church and the other musicians.

8. Use auditions. Contemporary services demand high quality music. So you will want to ensure that you use the best musicians possible. By announcing auditions you automatically have permission to say "yes" to some and "no" to others. And there will be those to whom you will have to say "no." For whatever reason, they may not fit into the group. Putting a group together consists of more than finding talented musicians. It also requires forming a cohesive team.

Certainly, you will want to use the audition to evaluate the talent of the musician. But you will also want to look into his or her heart. Why does this person want to be in the group? What is his or her relationship with God? Is this person truly committed to doing what it takes to put together a great group? Does he or she truly understand the mission and vision of the service and support

it? Does this person represent your church and the gospel well?

9. Take responsibility for choosing the music. Musical preference is extremely personal and highly emotional. Any group of musicians will have varying musical tastes. And if the group is left to choose the music, it could spell disaster. Arguments and hurt feelings can be the result. People take it personally if someone doesn't like the song they chose.

The person in charge of putting the service together should ultimately be responsible for choosing the music (that is, the music director or equivalent under the guidance of the pastor). You will want to use music that stylistically reaches the audience you have targeted. You will want that music to reflect the character of the church and the gospel as you understand it. You will also want to be certain that the words adequately express what you want to say. While the group will certainly want some say in what they sing, the mission of the service, the theology of the church, and the target audience will determine your musical choices—not personal taste.

10. Don't start a contemporary praise service until you have the group firmly in place. If the musicians or the sound of the group is not what you want, then delay the implementation of the service. In most settings where contemporary worship will be seen as suspect, you will get one chance to make it work. If the service bombs, you may not get a chance to try it again for years. So make sure everything, especially the music, is right and ready to go.

Getting the Sound Right

DAVE HORN

It's time for your contemporary praise service to begin. Much forethought has gone into its planning. You understand who you are trying to reach; music and sermon titles have an integrated theme; the order of worship has been established—but you find that you cannot count on your sound system to perform in a predictable manner. Nothing adds to the flow of worship in a more understated way than a system that operates unnoticed. On the flip side, nothing detracts from a service more quickly than a system that screeches and rasps.

How to Buy Equipment

Your church can purchase equipment from many different sources. These sources include the local music or audio store, professional sound system contractors, and mail-order operations. Technically adept, worship-sensitive people work in all these types of companies. Do not make a major purchase with the feeling that you have few, if any, good options. You can choose from hundreds of vendors. Be aware, however, that all forms of purchasing have advantages and disadvantages.

The local audio store. The strengths of a local store include its ability to respond quickly to problems, a stocked showroom in which to audition equipment, loaner equipment if you have a service problem, and a local resource person if you need an on-site visit. You can also generally expect more personalized service from a local retailer. Local stores, however, may not carry the broad range of professional products that will meet the unique needs of the church offered by a sound contractor or high-end mail-order operation. In some instances, your local store may be more accustomed to dealing with night club bands and may be truly unfamiliar with the requirements of the modern church. Even many equipment manufacturers do not understand the need for professional audio products in the church. Too often, equipment displayed in stores is done so in a manner different from any "real-world" setting. Further, the level of installation expertise may not be adequate if the store is used to selling mainly portable PA systems.

The professional contractor. Hiring a professional sound system contractor is your most expensive short-term alternative. However, a sound contractor is usually less expensive in terms of reliable long-term service, getting a properly designed system, and professional installation. You will pay more to have a system rightly installed, but you should be able to expect trouble-free service lasting many years. Most reliable contractors have made significant investments in design and analysis equipment. In addition, they are members of the National Systems Contractors Association (NSCA) or similar professional organizations, and/or have a significant level of professional training and experience.

Mail-order systems. You can save money if you know where to shop for equipment through merchants who use catalogs and/or toll-free numbers. A growing number of mail-order companies offer a very high level of technical advice and expertise, but be cautious because not all can or do. Many companies simply have people answering the phones to take orders. If you choose to use a mail-order company, find

one that has a staff with real-world experience and an understanding of worship. You want to be able to trust their recommendations for products with which you are not familiar.

If you live in a rural area with limited choices, look for a company in a nearby metropolitan area. Companies in these cities are better able to stock a broader product range due to the size of their market. A large variety of selections helps increase the chance of finding the product(s) you need for your particular situation. If you do not know where to start, make a few telephone calls to other churches near you and ask questions.

How to Determine Your Needs

When designing a sound system you should be prepared to answer the following questions or to give this information to your audio dealer of choice. Do not hesitate to invite a representative from your local dealer to attend one of your church services. An understanding of your style of worship is essential to his or her effectiveness at making good recommendations to you. This group of questions forces a church to think about its current situation by forecasting growth and future changes. Buying intelligently helps you better manage the resources that God has entrusted to you.

1. List the dimensions of your worship room and platform area. Do you have a balcony? How high is your ceiling? Is it vaulted? A videotape, photographs, and/or architect's drawings are ideal.

2. What is the seating capacity of this worship room? How many currently attend your largest weekly service?

3. What type of seating (chairs, pews) do you use?

4. What are the surface coverings of the walls, floors, ceiling, and pews? (Specify for each.)

5. Is the room used for any nonworship purpose (sports, banquets, classes)? Is this facility temporary or permanent? Do (or will) you set up and tear down the sound system for each service?

6. What is your congregation's style of music and worship? Do you like to "feel" the music? Is the primary source of music taped accompaniment, live musicians, or both? If you use live music, what is your instrumentation? Do you use electronic musical instruments other than an organ?

7. Do you desire a stage monitoring and/or hearing assistance system?

8. How many mixer input channels do you need? Count microphones, tape decks, CD players, instruments, effects units, and so on. Allow up to 50 percent more input channels if you expect to grow.

9. Is there a specific area where you wish to locate the mixer and related electronic equipment? If so, where?

10. If replacing a sound system: How old is the existing wiring for speakers and electronics? Do you currently have enough microphone and speaker jacks for this new equipment?

11. What type of sound equipment do you currently own?

12. Do you hope to use any of this equipment in the new system? If so, what?

13. What are your plans for building expansion and growth in membership in the next year? The next five years?

14. Does a separate electrical circuit exist for the sound system? If so, how many amperes?

15. How much money do you plan to budget for these improvements? Do you require financing?

After answering these questions you will be more prepared to take on the challenge of buying the proper equipment for your church. Professional sound equipment is not inexpensive and your cheapest alternative is not usually your best. You must also take into consideration your own level of expertise. If your church requires more assistance from a dealer, expect to pay for it in terms of higher prices. In return, your dealer should provide you the training and service that you need.

Please do not unfairly use your local retailer's time only to buy from a mail-order source because it is less expensive. And by all means, do not expect any retailer to answer questions about equipment purchased from another source.

Buying and using a sound system in a church can be a positive experience for all involved. Consult with different sources, be prepared to answer the questions that a good retailer will ask, be fair in your expectations, and treat your dealer in the same manner that you expect to be treated. It's not always how much money you save, but how well the job gets done!

Dave Horn is the president of Truth Seeker Productions in Columbus, Ohio. Truth Seeker Productions specializes in helping your worship services sound and look better through the use of properly applied professional sound, lighting, and video equipment. If you have questions related to a technical situation in your church or would like to speak with someone regarding system design, please feel free to call Truth Seeker at (800) 747-7301.

Tips for Sound Techs Who Work with Worship Leaders

DAVE HORN

1. Keep in mind that both you and the worship leader have the same goal—to make the worship service flow as smoothly as possible.

2. Work hard. When possible, arrive early to ensure that the sound system is working properly before it is needed.

3. Know your equipment and what it can and cannot do. Do not hesitate to explain that certain requests are not possible given the constraints of your system.

4. It is the worship leader's responsibility to make certain that the overall worship service flows well. Your excellence will make his or her job easier.

5. Pay attention during worship services and rehearsals. Nothing is more bothersome than a sound tech whose mind is elsewhere.

6. The best compliment to your efforts is no compliment at all. Do not be discouraged by a lack of praise for your job. The sound system, after all, is best when unnoticeable.

7. Be open to constructive criticism. Do not place a defensive barrier between your worship leader and yourself. Often, sound system operators can become overly comfortable or satisfied in their methods.

8. Do not be afraid of change. New technical ideas can freshen the worship experience.

9. Attend every worship team rehearsal possible. Try new ideas then—not on Sunday morning.

10. Worship Leaders: Your sound tech is an artist, too. Her or his ideas on how things should sound may differ from yours. Offer comments in a positive manner, remembering that your sound engineer is likely a volunteer.

Dave Horn is a consultant from Columbus, Ohio. He can be reached through Truth Seeker Productions, Inc. at (800) 747-7301. Reprinted with permission from Worship Leader, **Sept./Oct. 1995, Copyright © CCM Communications, Inc., Nashville, Tennessee.**

Resource Kit 2

CONTEMPORARY PRAISE SERVICES

Notes: This kit includes *two sample services*, *two sample sermons*, *a listing of worship chorus sources*, and *a chart of selected worship choruses*. This chart is not meant to be exhaustive. New choruses and resources are being released almost weekly. All the choruses listed would work well in a Contemporary Praise format. Many of the choruses included in this chart are available in several sources other than the ones listed. The copyright information is on the song, not the source. Most of the choruses listed can also be found on recordings. Check with your local Christian bookstore for more information.

The choral pieces from these sample services can be found in the chart provided in the Resource Kit in part 2. The small group songs can be found in the charts in the Resource Kit in part 4.

> **Key**
> 　* = appropriate for Spirited-Traditional services
> ** = appropriate for Seeker services
> 　S = slow tempo
> 　M = medium tempo
> 　F = fast tempo
> MS = moderately slow tempo
> MF = moderately fast tempo

CONTEMPORARY PRAISE AND WORSHIP SERVICE

Sermon Series

Building a Life that Counts—
PART ONE

Why Am I Here?

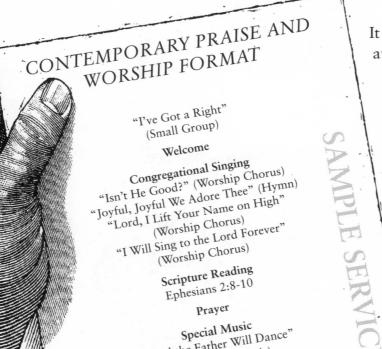

CONTEMPORARY PRAISE AND WORSHIP FORMAT

SAMPLE SERVICE

"I've Got a Right"
(Small Group)

Welcome

Congregational Singing
"Isn't He Good?" (Worship Chorus)
"Joyful, Joyful We Adore Thee" (Hymn)
"Lord, I Lift Your Name on High"
(Worship Chorus)
"I Will Sing to the Lord Forever"
(Worship Chorus)

Scripture Reading
Ephesians 2:8-10

Prayer

Special Music
"And the Father Will Dance"
(Celebration Choir)

Announcements/Offering

Special Music
(Sung while the offering is taken.
The offering is not returned
to the altar.)
"When I Am Gone"
(Small Group)

Message
"Why Am I Here?"

**Closing Prayer/The Lord's Prayer/
Benediction**

EPHESIANS 2:8-10

You are a masterpiece. Do you believe that? It must be true. God tells you that you were created as a piece of art. A masterpiece. You are God's workmanship. If you see some of the great works of art, some of the masterpieces in different parts of the world, you stand back in awe and think of the master. As that masterpiece was developed, you wonder, "How could they have done this?"

One summer in Laguna Beach, California we went to an evening performance that we happened to stumble upon. At a local festival of the arts, we saw recreations of masterpieces that come to life! People literally step out from the pictures.

Today we're going to talk about how to be God's masterpieces come alive. But before we do, let's have a word of prayer.

If you happen to end up in my office sometime, you'll see this *(holding up a framed document)* editorial letter written by George Bernard Shaw. He writes, "This is a true joy in life. The being used for a purpose. Recognized by yourself as a mighty one. The being a force of nature instead of a feverish selfish little clod with ailments and grievances, complaining that the world will not devote itself to making you happy. I am of the opinion that my life belongs to the whole community. And as long as I live it, it is my privilege to do for it whatever I can. I want to be thoroughly used up when I die. For the harder I work, the more I live. I rejoice in life for its own sake, for life is no brief candle to me. It is a sort of splendid torch which I got a hold of for the moment. And I want to make it burn as brightly as possible before handing it to future generations."

Many of you do not feel that you are a masterpiece. You don't feel like a torch. Maybe you feel like a firefly or a little match, a spark. Maybe even the spark is gone. Well, today there is a word for you from God. We don't want to miss it. The truth is this from the Bible passage we're focusing on: That when we picture ourselves as God pictures us, we are to be that and become that. Picture yourself as God pictures you. A masterpiece. A burning torch.

The Army commercial tells us, "Join the Army and be all that you can be!" Well, the Army can't do it for us. Positive motivational speakers say that you can do it on your own if you only think positive. Well, I believe in positive thinking. But positive thinking outside of God is empty; it is vanity. But we can make our lives count because each one of us is a masterpiece. Let's think about that.

Because you are a masterpiece, you can make a difference. Our young people went to Hawaii on a mission trip. Many of you heard the reports—they were phenomenal. Here were many teenagers who pictured their lives as God pictured them and then they became that—they lived that picture out as they went on this mission. They went into human services institutions. There they saw people who were strung out on drugs. People who had failed miserably. People who had been in prison. Hardened criminals. As our young people began to present what God believed to be true about them, they made a difference. These hardened criminals started to cry. Grown men with frozen faces started to melt. They caught a glimpse of what God saw them to be. The teenagers provide proof that we are here to help people discover that they are a masterpiece.

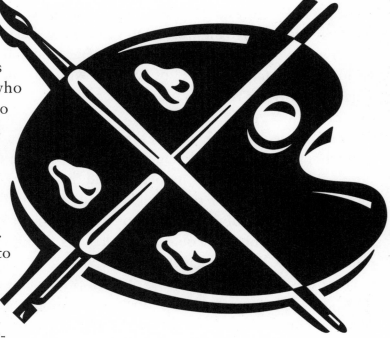

Our young people also went into a church. The night before, an unchurched man had a dream. He dreamed that he was going to be saved by a hundred raindrops—that somehow he was going to be rescued by a hundred raindrops. He had no idea what that meant. His wife was in church. He was at home. She went home to get him after she heard the musical presentation by our youth. She brought her husband to the next service. As he listened to our young people it became clear to him that the hundred raindrops were these teenagers who were making a difference. He invited and welcomed Jesus Christ into his life. His life was changed forever. Our teens were a torch sharing the love of Christ.

Because we are a masterpiece we can reach our fullest potential, and that sets us free to make a difference.

Sweet Alice was in jail when she was twelve years old. She wasn't so sweet. At thirteen Sweet Alice ended up pregnant and had a child. When Sweet Alice was fifteen she was homeless. As she sat on the street believing herself to be a miserable failure (her life certainly wasn't a torch) a woman named Ann Cowman, a Jewish woman, looked into Sweet Alice's eyes and said, "Young woman, you have a million dollar smile." Alice looked up. Ann had her attention.

Ann continued: "The world needs that million dollar smile and I'm going to see that you bring it to the world. I'm going to bring that smile out of you." Ann was telling her that she was going to help Alice reach her full God-given potential.

You know what happened? Sweet Alice won the Hero of America award in 1993. She went on to organize Parents of Watts. She is out making a difference. She is maximizing the potential God placed in her. She is becoming the masterpiece God created her to be.

We can certainly make a difference. We can reach our fullest potential as we picture ourselves as God pictures us. We are God's masterpiece.

We can also change the world. Do you believe that? If you don't believe it, you won't become it. You won't do it. If you don't believe what God believes about you, that you can change the world, you'll come to the end of your life with all that resource—all your potential left in you. That's not why we're here. We're here to change the world. But we don't do it on our own power.

Max Dupree is probably one of the most insightful leadership gurus in the world. He tells a story about his little granddaughter, Zoe. *Zoe* is the Greek word for life. Zoe was born two months premature. The neonatologist told the Duprees that the baby would not live. The baby only weighed 1 pound 7 ounces. The family went into the neonatology unit and saw the little baby covered with tubes. A respirator was attached to her. There were needles in her stomach. Max talks about how he could have taken his wedding ring and put it up the entire arm of his granddaughter; she was that small.

There was a nurse by the name of Ruth. Ruth came up to Max and his wife Esther and said, "O.K., now. You're going to be Zoe's surrogate parents. You are going to go in every day and after you have sterilized yourselves you're going to take your little finger and gently stroke little Zoe. And as you are stroking her, tell her how much you love her. Tell the baby how much God loves her. Tell that little baby that she is special, that she has a fantastic future." She went on to say, "What you need to do is to connect the voice with the touch. You need to connect voice and touch so that the baby will be able to grow, survive, and reach her maximum potential."

When we realize that we are God's workmanship, that we are God's work of art, that we are created in the image of God, we reach our potential. And then we're able to connect the world with the voice and touch of God. That's why we're here. That's what life is all about. That's how we reach our fullest potential. That's how we make our lives count. That's how we change the world.

Here is a popular poem that fits our theme for today. It reads:

'Twas battered and scarred, and the auctioneer
Thought it scarcely worth his while
To waste much time on the old violin,
But he held it up with a smile.
"What am I bidden, good folks," he cried,
"Who'll start the bidding for me?"
"A dollar, a dollar," then, "Two!" "Only two?
Two dollars and who'll make it three?
Three dollars once; three dollars twice;
Going for three, . . ." But no,
From the room, far back, a gray-haired man
Came forward and picked up the bow;
Then, wiping the dust from the old violin,
and tightening the loose strings,
He played a melody pure and sweet
As a caroling angel sings.

The music ceased, and the auctioneer,
With a voice that was quiet and low,
Said, "What am I bid for the old violin?"
And he held it up with the bow.
"A thousand dollars, and who'll make it two?
Two thousand! And who'll make it three?
Three thousand, once; three thousand, twice,
And going, and gone," said he.
The people cheered, but some of them cried,
"We do not quite understand
What changed its worth." Swift came the reply:
"The touch of a master's hand."

And many a man with life out of tune,
And battered and scarred with sin,
Is auctioned cheap to the thoughtless crowd,
Much like the old violin.
A "mess of pottage," a glass of wine;
A game—and he travels on.
He is "going" once, and "going" twice,
He's "going" and almost "gone."

But the Master comes, and the foolish crowd
Never can quite understand
The worth of a soul and the change that's wrought
By the touch of the Master's hand.

                              Myra Brooks Welch, 1936

Are you willing to let the master who created you as a masterpiece touch and transform your life? Are you willing to picture yourself as God pictures you today and then be that? That's what God intends for us. That's how life becomes all that we long for it to be. That's how we build a life that counts.

This message was preached during a contemporary praise service by Walt Kallestad, senior pastor of Community Church of Joy in Glendale, Arizona.

CONTEMPORARY PRAISE AND WORSHIP COMMUNION SERVICE
Sermon Series

Building a Life that Counts—
PART TWO

Building on My Strengths

PSALM 139:13-14

If you ever have encountered a mechanism that makes you feel insignificant or that demotivates you, then you have tried "voice mail." Imagine that you are witnessing a tragedy and you find yourself in a 911 voice mail system: *(Pick up telephone handset; telephone touch tones are captured through the sound system.)*

"Thank you for calling 911. In order to serve you better your call is being routed to the police department, fire department, hospital, or mortuary best able to help you. If your home is being broken into, press 1. If the intruder is armed, press 2. If the intruder is in the room from which you're making the call, press 4. If you are attempting to avoid detection and have turned off the lights press 2339200976 followed by the pound (#) sign. . . . I'm sorry, that is not a valid entry. Please try again.

"If you've been attacked since your last choice, are dazed, or unable to recall long strings of random numbers, press 1. If you're bleeding, press 4. If you're bleeding all over the rug, press 5. If you would like the number

CONTEMPORARY PRAISE AND WORSHIP COMMUNION FORMAT

"We're Gonna Lift Up His Name"
(Celebration Choir)

Welcome

Congregational Singing
"Celebrate Jesus, Celebrate" (Worship Chorus)
"Great Is the Lord" (Worship Chorus)

Scripture Reading
Psalm 139:13-14

Prayer

Special Music
"Runner" (Celebration Choir)

Announcements/Offering

Special Music
(Sung during the offering.
The offering is not brought back to the altar.)
"I Know Where I Stand" (Small Group)

Message
"Building on My Strengths"

Celebration of Communion
Prayer of Confession
(informal or from denominational hymnal)
The Lord's Prayer
Words of Institution

Congregational Singing
(during communion)
"Wonderful Counselor"
"Change My Heart, O God"
"Holy Ground" (Worship Choruses)

Communion Blessing / Benediction

SAMPLE SERVICE

of a good cleaner, press 7. If you want more options, press 1776* in honor of the choices opened up by the American Revolution. If you want to know the choices of other states, press 1776 followed by the number of stars indicating the order in which the state was admitted into the Union. For a listing of the order of admission press 3. To repeat this message, press 2. If you're still bleeding, press down hard on the wound."

There are many things in life that make us feel insignificant and that demotivate us. A hundred things can go right. And one thing can go wrong. What do we focus on? We can be strong in many areas of our life and be weak in one area. What do we spend our time concentrating on?

Jackie Smith was a professional football player a number of years ago. He was on the road to the Hall of Fame until one thing happened. In 1976 the Dallas Cowboys and the Pittsburgh Steelers were in the Super Bowl. Jackie Smith used one of his patented moves on a defender and found himself wide open in the end zone. Roger Staubach floated a beautiful pass right into Jackie's jersey numbers. But somehow Jackie blew it. The ball bounced off his hands and fell onto the ground. And Dallas lost the game. Twenty years later what do people talk about? Whenever Jackie Smith is on a talk show, a replay is run showing him dropping the pass and losing the game for his team. It's really tragic that we have somehow made a decision to focus on failure. We can certainly learn from failure. But we are not to lean on failure.

On the other side of that, the Chinese have won the Olympic Ping Pong Championship forever. A film was scripted about them called, *Soaring with Your Strengths.* This documentary interviewed the Chinese coach. The interviewer tried to find out why these world class athletes continually win the championship. You know what the coach said? "We spend eight hours a day building on their strengths."

For example, the Chinese Olympic champion of 1984 had a terrible backhand. Some coaches would have taken that weakness, blown the weakness up by working too hard on it, and in the process would have virtually overlooked the potential in this champion. But what this Chinese coach did instead was focus on the strength of the forehand. And he built the forehand so that it became invincible. It could not be beaten.

The Bible contains a story that is based on a similar principle. David, who is the subject of Psalm 139, confronted a giant named Goliath. Goliath was a big bulky, Arnold Schwarzenegger type—intimidating. He'd call across the battle line to the Israelites: "You wimps! We're going to wipe you out. You're nothing! We're going to destroy you!" David heard Goliath's challenge: "I dare someone to come out and fight me."

David was a little scrawny guy. But he knew how to use a slingshot. David was a shepherd. The shepherd would use the slingshot when wild animals would come and try to destroy the sheep. David was a master with the slingshot. It was his strength. Though he wasn't bulky and strong like Goliath, he had a different kind of strength than the giant. David said to the Israelites standing around him, "This battle is the Lord's. And with God I can defeat the giant."

That kind of self-confidence reminds us of Sir Hillary, the great mountain climber. Hillary was asked, "How do you climb these huge mountains?" He responded, "I don't conquer the mountain. I conquer myself and them I am able to get up the mountain."

David conquered himself. He focused on his strengths and was able to take his slingshot and nail Goliath right between the eyes. The big giant went toppling over.

We each have been given incredible strengths. And God wants us to build on them by acknowledging them.

There are various kinds of strengths. Some people have strengths of communication. They are able to speak very articulately. They are able to sum something up in a practical, understandable way. They are very motivating. They are encouraging. What they say or write makes an impact. Their communication strengths are a gift and they can be enhanced.

There's another kind of strength. There's an analytical strength. There are people who can take a situation and analyze it. They love to analyze. They're detail people. If you were to go into their garages you might see all the tools lined up on the wall very neatly. If you were to go into their kitchens you might find the spices sitting in alphabetical order. Very detailed and very neat. Those are strengths.

There are also people with sensing strengths. Our daughter has an incredible gift of sensitivity. When somebody is hurting she senses it and is very empathetic, open, and helpful.

There are people who have directing strengths. They are in charge. They come to a meeting and help put together a blueprint or plan and lead the change. They lead the way. They have gifts of directing. They should focus on those strengths and build on them.

The Bible tells us that we are wonderfully made. Every single person has strengths, and we're called to build the life God intends for us by using those strengths. We do that by acknowledging them.

But before you make a list of personal strengths, remember that we build a life that counts by affirming the strengths of others.

Sister Merosula, a teacher in Morris, Minnesota, had a class of thirty-four third graders. One of her students, Mark, was a nonstop talker. (A kid with verbal skills!) He chatted all the time and disrupted everything. Finally, one day, she was fed up. She said, "Mark, you open your mouth one more time and I'm going to tape it shut!"

So now the class became police officers. They carefully watched Mark, hoping that he would open his mouth. Sure enough, it wasn't but a few seconds later that Mark started chattering again. Sister Merosula got the tape, went over, and put a big X on Mark's mouth. Of course, the class was giggling. This was a big deal. She went to sit down and then looked up to make sure that Mark was O.K. When she looked at him, he winked at her. She lost it. She started laughing. The whole class started laughing so she went over and took the tape off Mark. And Mark said, "Thank you, Sister, for correcting me." Well, Sister Merosula couldn't help but love Mark. He was a lovable kid.

In seventh grade, Sister Merosula once again had Mark in her class. The seventh graders were learning some very difficult math. It was the middle of the year, spirits were low, and everybody was cranky and grouchy. One Friday afternoon Sister Merosula said, "All right.

Take out a sheet of clean paper." The students found the paper. "On that sheet of paper I want you to write every student's name down." So they did. Then she said, "Now, next to their names, I want you to write one thing you really like about each person." So every student took time to write about the other students. They affirmed one another.

The following Monday Sister Merosula came with a card for every student with their name on it. On it were the comments written by the other students saying what they liked about the person. The attitude of the class changed dramatically. Spirits soared. People cared for one another again.

But that's not the end of the story. Mark grew up. He went off to Vietnam and was killed there. Mark's parents invited Sister Merosula to the funeral. After the service they pulled her aside. They handed her Mark's wallet. Inside she found a tattered, torn, taped together, floppy piece of paper and on it was written all the things that his classmates liked about him when they were in seventh grade. You can imagine, from the wear and tear, how often Mark referred to that list. His parents said to Sister Merosula, "We want you to have this. Mark treasured it. And we want you to have his treasure."

We are called by God to affirm the strengths of our children, our neighbors, and our work associates. We are called to find what they are doing right and encourage them and affirm them. That's how God intends for us to live out our lives.

By applying this principle a man actually saved his son's life. A woman, Holice Bridges, operates an institute in California. She makes blue ribbons that read in gold, "Who I Am Makes a Difference." She pins the ribbon next to a person's heart and then gives that person two ribbons to pass along to others to encourage them. One day a young executive got a ribbon pinned on him in one of Holice Bridges's seminars. When returning to his office he thought, "You know, a lot of people think my supervisor is grumpy, grouchy, and mean. But I'm going to give him one of these." So he went to his boss and said, "Sir, thank you for your work. You're very innovative. I want you to have this." He put the ribbon on his boss. "And here's one to give to someone else."

The senior boss, as he was driving home, thought about who he should honor with the ribbon. He thought about his son. As he went into his home he said, "Son, I want to see you for a few moments in private." They went into a room and sat down. "Son, I've been thinking about who I wanted to honor today. I know I haven't paid too much attention to you lately, but Son, I love you, and I want to honor you. Who you are makes a difference." He then pinned the ribbon on him.

His son started to sob. He started to shake. He wept uncontrollably. Dad reached out and held him. And then his son looked up through his tear-filled eyes and said, "Dad, I guess I won't commit suicide today."

Dad's words to his son were actually words from God. We can make a difference by making a phone call or writing a letter. Or by letting someone know as we affirm their strengths that they can make a difference.

Two thousand years ago Jesus came to affirm our strengths—to let us know how much God loves and values us. He came to remind us that we are wonderfully made. That God created us with special strengths and talents. And as you acknowledge those strengths and build on them, as you affirm the strengths in others, as you see yourself through the eyes of Jesus, you will discover the joy of building a life that counts.

This message was preached during a contemporary praise service by Walt Kallestad, senior pastor of Community Church of Joy, in Glendale, Arizona.

PRAISE CHORUS RESOURCES

"All Hail, King Jesus"* (MS)
Words and Music: Dave Moody
Copyright © 1981 Glory Alleluia Music
Songs for Praise and Worship
Worship Planner Edition

"Amazing Grace"* (M)
Words and Music: John Newton/American Melody
Maranatha! Music Praise Chorus Book

"Bless the Lord,
O My Soul"* (M)
Words and Music: Unknown
Copyright © 1992 Word Music
Songs for Praise and Worship
Worship Planner Edition

"Blessed Be the Name
of the Lord" (M)
Words and Music: Dan Moen
Copyright © 1986 Integrity's Hosanna! Music
Praise and Worship Songbook One
Hosanna! Integrity Music

"Celebrate Jesus"* (F)
Words and Music: Gary Oliver
Copyright © 1988/1992 Integrity's Hosanna!
  Music
Songs for Praise and Worship
Worship Planner Edition

"Change My Heart,
O God"* (MS)
Words and Music: Kelly Willard
Copyright © 1982 Maranatha! Music/Willing Heart
  Music
Maranatha! Music Praise Chorus Book
Expanded 2nd Edition

"Come into
His Presence" (MF)
Words and Music: Lynn Baird
Copyright © 1983/1992 Integrity's Hosanna! Music
Songs for Praise and Worship
Worship Planner Edition

"Come, Let Us Sing for
Joy"** (F)
Words and Music: Brent Chambers
Copyright © 1984 Scripture in Song
Praise and Worship Songbook Two
Hosanna! Integrity Music

"Cry of My Heart"** (MF)
Words and Music: Terry Butler
Copyright © 1992, 1993 Mercy Publishing
Let the Walls Fall Down—Praise Band 4

"Emmanuel"* (MS)
Words and Music: Bob McGee
Copyright © 1976 C. A. Music
Maranatha! Music Praise Chorus Book

"Everlasting" (M)
Words and Music: Rick Founds
Copyright © 1990 Maranatha! Music
Everlasting—The Praise Band (3)

"Give Thanks"* (MS)
Words and Music: Henry Smith
Copyright © 1978 Integrity's Hosanna! Music
Praise and Worship Songbook Seven
Hosanna! Integrity Music

"Great Is the Lord"* (MS)
Words and Music: Michael W. Smith/Deborah D. Smith
Copyright © 1982/1992 Meadowgreen Music Co.
Songs for Praise and Worship
Worship Planner Edition

"Hallowed Be Thy Name"** (MF)
Words and Music: Babbie Mason/Robert Lawson
Copyright © 1988, 1990 Word Music
Everlasting—The Praise Band (3)

"He Is Able"* (MS)
Words and Music: Rory Noland/Greg Ferguson
Copyright © 1989 Maranatha! Music
You Are So Faithful—The Praise Band (2)

"He Is the King" (MF)
Words and Music: Tom Ewing/Don Moen/John Stocker
Copyright © 1989/1992 Integrity's Hosanna! Music
Songs for Praise and Worship
Worship Planner Edition

"Holy Ground"* (S)
Words and Music: Christopher Beatty
Copyright © 1979 Birdwing Music/Cherry Lane Music Pub.
Praise and Worship Songbook One
Integrity's Hosanna! Music

"Holy Ground"* (S)
Words and Music: Geron Davis
Copyright © 1983 Meadowgreen Music Co.
Praise and Worship Songbook One
Integrity's Hosanna! Music

"How Excellent Is Thy Name" (F)
Words and Music: Dave Tunney
Copyright © 1985/1992 BMG Songs, Inc.
Songs for Praise and Worship
Worship Planner Edition

"I Just Want to Praise You"* (MS)
Words and Music: Arthur Tannous
Copyright © 1984, 1987 Acts Music Admin.
Maranatha! Music Praise Chorus Book
Expanded 2nd Edition

"I Love You, Lord"* (S)
Words and Music: Laurie Klein
Copyright © 1978/1980 House of Mercy Music
Songs for Praise and Worship
Worship Planner Edition

"I Love Your Grace"** (F)
Words and Music: Rick Founds
Copyright © 1990 Maranatha! Music
Everlasting—The Praise Band (3)

"I Want to Thank You, Lord"** (MF)
Words and Music: Sue Rinaldi/Ray Goudie/Steve Bassett
Copyright © 1984 Word Music
You Are So Faithful—The Praise Band (2)

"I Will Celebrate"** (MF)
Words and Music: Rita Baloche
Copyright © 1990 Maranatha! Music
Praise and Worship Songbook Seven
Integrity's Hosanna! Music

"I Will Sing to the Lord Forever" (MF)

Words and Music: Joey Holder
Copyright © 1990 Integrity's Hosanna! Music
Praise and Worship Songbook Five
Integrity's Hosanna! Music

"I Worship You Almighty God"* (MS)

Words and Music: Sondra Corbett
Copyright © 1983 Integrity's Hosanna! Music
Praise and Worship Songbook One
Integrity's Hosanna! Music

"In His Time"* (S)

Words and Music: Diane Ball
Copyright © 1978/1983 Maranatha! Music
Maranatha! Music Praise Chorus Book

"Isn't He Good?"** (MF)

Words and Music: Beverly Darnall
Copyright © 1983 Maranatha! Music
Let the Walls Fall Down—Praise Band 4

"It Is Good to Praise the Lord"** (MS)

Words and Music: Lenny LeBlanc
Copyright © 1989 Doulos Publishing
You Are So Faithful—The Praise Band (2)

"Jesus, Name Above All Names"* (MS)

Words and Music: Naida Hearn
Copyright © 1974/1978 Scripture in Song
Maranatha! Music Praise Chorus Book

"Lord, Be Glorified (In My Life, Lord)"* (S)

Words and Music: Bob Kilpatrick
Copyright © 1978/1986 Prism Tree Music
Maranatha! Music Praise Chorus Book
Expanded 2nd Edition

"Lord, I Lift Your Name on High" (M)

Words and Music: Rick Founds
Copyright © 1989/1990 Maranatha! Music
Maranatha! Music Praise Chorus Book
Expanded 2nd Edition

"Mighty Is Our God" (F)

Words and Music: Eugene Greco/Gerrit Gustafson/
    Don Moen
Copyright © 1988/1992 Integrity's Hosanna! Music
Songs for Praise and Worship
Worship Planner Edition

"My Life Is in You, Lord" (F)

Words and Music: Daniel Gardner
Copyright © 1986/1992 Integrity's Hosanna!
    Music
Songs for Praise and Worship
Worship Planner Edition

"O Magnify the Lord" (M)

Words and Music: Michael O'Shields
Copyright © 1981 Sound III, Inc.
Songs for Praise and Worship
Worship Planner Edition

"Open Our Eyes, Lord"* (M)

Words and Music: Robert Cull
Copyright © 1976 Maranatha! Music
Songs for Praise and Worship
Worship Planner Edition

"Seek Ye First"* (M)

Words and Music: Karen Laferty
Copyright © 1972 Maranatha! Music
Songs for Praise and Worship
Worship Planner Edition

"Sing a Joyful Song"** (MF)

Rick Founds
Copyright © 1989 Maranatha! Music
You Are So Faithful—The Praise Band (2)

"Sing, Shout, Clap"** (F)
Words and Music: Billy Funk
Copyright © 1990 Integrity's Praise! Music
Praise and Worship Songbook Seven
Integrity's Hosanna! Music

"Sweet Jesus"** (F)
Words and Music: Traditional
Copyright © 1990 Maranatha! Music
Everlasting—The Praise Band (3)

"The Greatest Thing"* (MF)
Words and Music: Mark Pendergrass
Copyright © 1977/1983 Sparrow Song
Maranatha! Music Praise Chorus Book
Expanded 3rd Edition

"There Is Joy in the Lord"** (MF)
Words and Music: Cheri Keaggy
Copyright © 1993 Cheri Keaggy
Let the Walls Fall Down—Praise Band 4

"We Will Glorify"* (MS)
Words and Music: Twila Paris
Copyright © 1982 Singspiration Music
Songs for Praise and Worship
Worship Planner Edition

"We Worship and Adore You"* (M)
Words and Music: Tom Fettke
Copyright © 1992 Word Music
Songs for Praise and Worship
Worship Planner Edition

"What a Mighty God We Serve" (F)
Words and Music: Unknown
Copyright © 1986 Integrity's Hosanna! Music
Praise and Worship Songbook One
Integrity's Hosanna! Music

"White as Snow"* (MS)
Words and Music: Leon Olguin
Copyright © 1990/1992 Maranatha! Music
Maranatha! Music Praise Chorus Book
Expanded 3rd Edition

"Wonderful Counselor"* (M)
Words and Music: Bill Yeager
Copyright © 1982/1986 Maranatha! Music
Maranatha! Music Praise Chorus Book
Expanded 2nd Edition

"Worthy, You Are Worthy"* (M)
Words and Music: Don Moen
Copyright © 1986/1992 Integrity's Hosanna! Music
Songs for Praise and Worship
Worship Planner Edition

CHORUS SOURCE LIST

Let the Walls Fall Down—
Praise Band 4
Bob Somma, Jeff Larns, John Campbell
Copyright © 1993 Maranatha! Music

You Are So Faithful/
The Praise Band
John Schreiner, Bill Wolaver
Copyright © 1990 Maranatha! Music

Everlasting—
The Praise Band
John Andrew Schreiner, Bill Wolaver,
Danny Zaloudik
Copyright © 1990 Maranatha! Music

Maranatha!
Music Praise Chorus Book
not listed
Copyright © 1983 Maranatha! Music

Maranatha!
Music Praise Chorus Book—
Expanded 2nd Edition
C. Seal, G. Marestaing, T. Coomes, S. Endi-
cott, B. Owens, J. Bonilla
Copyright © 1990 Maranatha! Music

Maranatha!
Music Praise Chorus Book—
Expanded 3rd Edition
George Baldwin, Andrea Whittaker, Jo
Bonilla, Tommy Coomes
Copyright © 1993 Maranatha! Music

Songs for Praise
and Worship—
Worship Planner Edition
not listed
Copyright © 1992 Word Music

Praise and
Worship Songbook One
Jeff Hamlin, Tom Brooks
Copyright © 1987 Integrity Music, Inc.

Praise and
Worship Songbook Two
Dan Burgess
Copyright © 1988 Integrity Music, Inc.

Praise and
Worship Songbook Three
Dan Burgess
Copyright © 1989 Integrity Music, Inc.

Praise and Worship Songbook Four
Dan Burgess
Copyright © 1990 Integrity Music, Inc.

Praise and Worship Songbook Five
Dan Burgess
Copyright © 1991 Integrity Music, Inc.

Praise and Worship Songbook Six
Dan Burgess
Copyright © 1992 Integrity Music, Inc.

Praise and Worship Songbook Seven
Dan Burgess
Copyright © 1993 Integrity Music, Inc.

Praise and Worship Songbook Eight
Dan Burgess
Copyright © 1994 Integrity Music, Inc.

Praise and Worship Songbook Nine
Dan Burgess
Copyright © 1995 Integrity Music, Inc.

Part 4

CONTEMPORARY OUTREACH-ORIENTED SERVICES

*Contemporary Outreach-Oriented Services
seek to make worship culturally relevant
for those unfamiliar with Christianity,
the Bible, church tradition,
and traditional forms of worship.
These services emphasize outreach
and the presentation of the gospel.*

The Six W's of Contemporary Worship

TIM WRIGHT

When designing a contemporary worship service, you will want to consider the following six questions:

1. Why? Before launching a contemporary service a congregation will want to determine its motivation by asking, "Why do we want to offer this service? What is its purpose? What do we hope to accomplish?"

Contemporary worship, in and of itself, is not a cure for a declining congregation. It does not automatically produce growth in a congregation. Nor is contemporary worship appropriate for every church. Not every congregation has the resources to make such a change.

If the church wants to offer an alternative service because it seems to be the thing to do—because other congregations have had success with it—the service will never fly. The same disappointment appears if the primary motivation is to grow the church. If the motivation is misplaced, if the proper vision

is not kindled, the service will quickly die.

If, however, the congregation senses God's call to worship in this way, if the congregation believes it can more effectively reach new, unchurched people through this kind of worship, then the church has no choice but to go where God has called them to go.

2. What? The congregation will also ask, "What is the cost of this new service?" Many congregations have discovered that it takes a lot more work to offer a contemporary service than a denominationally oriented liturgical service. Many liturgical services come neatly packaged in a worship book. The order of service, the Bible passages, the prayers, and the hymns are right at one's fingertips. The basic pattern and form is set by decades or centuries of practice.

The same cannot be said of contemporary worship. Launching this new service will require as much energy and anxiety as launching or planting a new church. Contemporary services, while often following the same basic format week after week, are essentially recreated every week. Each week new choruses must be found. Volumes of books and CDs must be sifted through to find the appropriate special music. Dramas must be written. Contemporary worship requires an intensive effort and extensive people hours. But when it comes together, the work is worth it!

3. Who? Asking three "who" questions will help make the service a success:

Who will drive the service? Who will set the vision for it? Who will make sure that the service is doing what it was designed to do? In my opinion, the answer to this question is the senior pastor. If the pastor is not 100 percent behind the service, if she or he is not actually leading the way in implementing the service, the church should not even attempt it. Successful contemporary services are driven by pastors who are passionate about using new forms of worship to reach new kinds of people.

Who will manage the service? Who will find the music? Who will recruit the band members? Who will lead the singing? Who will rehearse the bands? While the pastor oversees the service, he or she will need someone excited about contemporary worship who will pull it all

together. This person should (1) share the same vision and passion for the service as the pastor; (2) be in tune with current music styles; and (3) be able to find talented musicians and mold them into a cohesive group

In other words, to ensure a quality service, the pastor needs a champion who will make it happen. This may be the current worship leader. Or it may be necessary to recruit a new leader for the new service.

While a growing number of classically trained musicians recognize the need for—and even endorse—alternative forms of worship, many of them feel ill-equipped to handle such a service. Their training and skills are not conducive to more contemporary forms of music. These valuable members of the worship team need to be reaffirmed and given permission to produce the best liturgical service possible. Adding a contemporary service should not in any way suggest a lack of appreciation for classical/traditional expressions of worship. Nor should it devalue those who enjoy and participate in those kinds of services. Because many classically trained musicians feel uncomfortable with contemporary music, adding a person to the team who is more adept at contemporary

YOU'RE INVITED

styles may prove necessary. Though the classical musician and the contemporary musician will lead completely different styles of worship, they are not in competition. They serve on the same team, looking to accomplish the same goal, making the gospel and worship accessible to all people no matter what their musical preference.

Whom will the service target? Will the service be geared to believers or to seekers? Will the service seek to meet the needs of baby boomers (those born between 1946 and 1964) or the generation after them? The style of the music and the style of the service will be determined by the answers to those kinds of questions.

4. Where? The place of worship is as important as the style of worship. And the answer to the question, "Where will we hold the service?" is not always automatically the sanctuary. Some sanctuaries, due to their design, are not conducive to contemporary forms of worship. The acoustics can't handle the drums and guitars. The overall feeling of the building is too formal. And it may be that, at least to begin, the room is too big. An almost empty room creates a feeling of isolation and defeat among the persons attending.

Many churches have found the use of a fellowship hall or gymnasium to be more friendly to contemporary worship. Such rooms lend themselves to informality and encourage a certain amount of intimacy.

5. When? On what day will the service be held? Sunday? Saturday? Friday? The needs of the target audience will help make this decision.

At what time will it be offered? Early Sunday morning? (Not a good idea!) Mid-Sunday morning? The last service on Sunday morning? Sunday night? (Only if you want to satisfy existing believers.) Saturday night at 6:00? Saturday night at 10:00? Again, the target audience should be taken seriously when setting service times.

6. Word? How will we get the word out? How will we let our target audience know about the service? Two answers come to mind:

- *Advertise.* Some congregations mail out attractive flyers announcing the service. Some advertise using slides on movie screens between shows. Others buy ads in the newspaper or on radio and/or TV. But be aware that advertising can be expensive and does not usually get a high return on investment.
- *Use your members.* The fastest growing congregations emerge because their members invite their friends. As members see that the service is dynamic, exciting, relevant, and nonthreatening, they will enthusiastically invite others. One church surveyed their congregation and discovered that 81 percent of their members invite at least one friend to church each year! That's customer satisfaction!

An effective contemporary service requires a lot of planning, prayer, preparation, and persistence. But when the pieces are in place, it can add a whole new dimension and excitement to the ministry.

Building the Service Around a Theme

TIM WRIGHT

Effective services no longer depend solely on the sermon to get the point across. Instead, effective services today, particularly those used as outreach, use all the elements of the service to relevantly and dynamically share the theme or topic. The sermon, usually renamed a "message," serves as one piece in the puzzle.

For example, if the message title is, "How to Discover My God-Given Potential," the music, the drama, and the message will all focus on that topic. Perhaps the special music will explain how God created us in God's image. Maybe the drama will show several people trying to discover their unique gifts and talents in a humorous way. And tying it all together, the sermon might focus on Psalm 139, which expresses how we are fearfully and wonderfully made. Over and over again, through the music, drama, and message, the theme is held up and extended. I find it extremely helpful to mention the theme for the day at the beginning of the ser-

vice. Our church also lists the theme of the day at the top of the worship brochure. (And next week's theme is named too.) This helps people focus on what we're about. In worship services geared to the unchurched in particular, the entire service presents the message, not just the sermon.

Choosing Themes and Message Topics

Effective themes are relevant themes. They deal with real-life issues and share how the gospel speaks to them. In the past twenty years the majority of denominational pastors have used the lectionary to plan sermons. The lectionary was originally intended to guide the congregation in the public reading of Scripture. It offers a prescribed series of biblical texts that walk a congregation through the Bible in three years. Pastors seized an opportunity to use these texts as the thematic structure for their worship. Lectionary-oriented messages begin with the text and move to the audience. The lectionary is an excellent tool when preparing messages for the committed.

Theme-oriented messages, on the other hand, begin with the audience, and move to the text. Oftentimes, to build momentum, the theme will encompass a four- to seven-week series of messages. Each sermon shares a piece of that theme. For instance, a series of messages on midlife crisis could be entitled, "Building a Life that Counts." The sermon topics might include, "Defining My Mission in Life," "Building on My Strengths," "How to Renew the Dream," and "When All I Have Is All There Is."

The choice of relevant series themes and sermon topics can be a daunting task if you don't know where to look. Several suggestions for finding relevant themes include:

- Hanging out with nonchurchgoing people, listening to their hurts, concerns, questions, and doubts
- The self-help section of the local bookstore
- *USA Today* Life Section
- Bestseller lists (spirituality and angels are hot topics right now)
- Books and articles on culture and society (the baby boom and baby bust generations; trend shifts—moving from an industrial society to a knowledge society implications; and so on)
- Listening to the needs of your congregation—their struggles with parenting, work, marriage, divorce, illness, and so on
- Local newspapers

When creating the series theme and the message topics, aim for creative titles that grab people where they live. Most people won't pay attention to "An Exegetical Look at the Existential Symbols in Job." But listeners will be captivated by the theme: "Fit Living for Fast Times" fleshed out with messages on "Managing Stress," "Managing Your Emotions," and "Managing Your Time."

Once you've chosen your series theme and message topics, the next step is to choose the scripture passage. Perhaps a familiar text will come to mind. A computer concordance will speed up the search for an appropriate passage. Certainly this process can lead to proof-testing or preaching on one's favorite verses. But the aim of this kind of preaching and worship, in an outreach-oriented service, is not to offer technical theological studies on the nature of God or the Bible. The point is to connect the gospel to where people are living. The purpose is to introduce people to the concept that the Bible and the gospel do have something that is relevant to real, present-day life. Consider this process as "gospel preaching," rather than a large group Bible study.

By way of illustration, take the series theme, "How to Build Healthy Relationships." The series might develop in four parts:

- Message No. 1: "Building Healthy Relationships" (Mark 1:40-42)
- Message No. 2: "Commitment: The Key to Healthy Relationships" (John 15:12-13)
- Message No. 3: "How to Resolve Conflict" (Matt. 18:15-20)
- Message No. 4: "How to Be the Right Life Mate" (1 Cor. 13:1-8*a*)

Notice how the theme and the corresponding messages utilize little, if any, religious language. They speak to people in relevant, contemporary terms. But as the message is written, based on the chosen text, it will look at these topics from a Christian and biblical viewpoint.

Once the series theme and message topics are chosen, they can then be given to the music and drama directors, so that they can find the appropriate music and skits. Sometimes it's difficult to find music that fits a particular message topic. At that point, a song that fits the overall series theme will prove appropriate. (For more on this see "Writing the Service as a Team" on page 133.)

Once mixed together, the music, drama and/or interview, and the message will firmly plant the message for the day in the hearts and minds of the listeners.

Writing the Service as a Team

JAN WRIGHT

Creating an excellent outreach-oriented contemporary worship service requires considerable forethought, planning, and teamwork. The following steps can help your team build an attractive service:

Step 1: Determine the team. Depending on who does what in the area of worship in your church, the worship team can consist of the following: the pastor, the music director (paid or volunteer), the accompanist or band/ensemble leader (paid or volunteer), the drama director (paid or volunteer), the guest interview coordinator (paid or volunteer), the message research team (volunteer), the newsletter/bulletin editor (paid or volunteer), and anyone else responsible for planning and implementing worship.

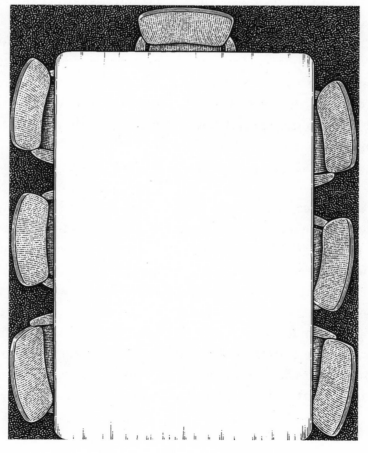

Step 2: Determine the format of the service. What will the format of the service look like? Will it be participational or presentational? What elements will we include in the service? Dramas? Interviews? Congregational singing? How and in what order will we use them? How long will the service last each week? Start out

with a sketch of the service order. The service should have a flow to it, without too much back-to-back talking. For example, scripture reading, followed by an interview, followed by announcements, followed by an introduction to the offering, and so on, is too many talking heads. When possible and appropriate, break up talking time with music to prevent loss of attention among the worshipers.

An outreach-oriented service might use the same basic format three weeks out of four. The services could include three special music slots (solos or small group performances), one worship chorus for audience participation, a special feature (drama or interview), a Bible reading and prayer, announcements and offering, and the message. By mixing up the form of the special feature from week to week—for example, interchanging dramas and interviews—the service remains fresh and the guests attentive. Occasionally at our church we will include some form of contemporary dance to add yet another dimension to the worship experience. One Sunday per month the same congregation could replace the special feature with Holy Communion. (See the format examples at the end of each section.)

Step 3: Decide on the service theme. Usually, the pastor will put together the message themes, titles, and Scripture passages. This should be done four to six months ahead of time. That information will direct the process of finding the music and dramas for the services. This list should go to the following people:

The music director. The music director, armed with the theme, can track down music and worship choruses that enhance that theme over and over again throughout the service. He or she then slots all the required music into the format. Occasionally it may prove difficult to find enough special numbers to match a particular theme. At those times make sure the song that does match the theme is placed where it fits best (for example, after the drama, or before the message).

For one service we had to find music to fit the theme, "Guilt-free Sex." Needless to say, there aren't many songs on that topic. We settled for something that talked about God's love. During a seminar on outreach-oriented worship, we mentioned our difficulty in finding a song to fit that theme. One United Methodist pastor suggested an old gospel solution: "Precious Memories"!

If a particular song (or a line from the drama) really captures the theme, let the pastor know. Sometimes the song or drama can be referred to in the sermon, which greatly adds to the cohesiveness of the service.

Once the music and choruses are chosen and reviewed with the rest of the worship team (see step 4) the music can be distributed to those who will be performing it. The more time they have to rehearse, the better!

- *The drama coordinator and/or the interview coordinator.* Drama functions as a parable. It helps people visualize the message and internalize it. It sets up the message. Drama can be humorous or poignant. It can either tell a story that reinforces what the pastor will say, or create a situation or question that will be answered in the message. To ensure the "flow" between music and drama, the music and drama directors will try to work together. For example, moving from a captivating, thought-provoking drama into a thoughtful, sensitive song can be very powerful. Sometimes it may be appropriate to move immediately into the music, thus disallowing applause. However, people usually like to respond with applause, so having the music set to start directly following can help make a nice "package." If the drama is particularly intense, the music may be used to help pull the mood back up. Be aware of what music and drama do emotionally. Always ask, "What message do we want to communicate? What mood do we want to set?" You might even try using drama directly before the message occasionally to help set up the message.

The interview can also coordinate with the theme if the person conducting the interview asks the right questions. For example, if the topic is marriage, a couple could be interviewed on the secrets of their strong marriage. If the theme is on overcoming tough times, the athlete being interviewed might be asked, "How has Jesus Christ made a difference during your tough times?" Sometimes, due to the availability of the interviewee and the content of her or his story, the interview may not focus directly on the topic for the day. At that point the interview serves as a personal faith story.

- *The message research team.* This group of volunteers helps the pastor research the message. They look for information, data, or stories that can help enhance the effectiveness of the sermon.
- *The newsletter editor* will include upcoming message topics in the congregations' advertising and newsletters.

Once the service is written, provide a copy of it, along with necessary chorus words (with required copyright information), titles, names of performers, and service theme clearly written, to the bulletin coordinator. Depending on your church, this may or may not be the same as the newsletter editor.

Step 4: Meet with the worship team each week. This particular planning session includes anyone responsible for the actual implementation of the service (the pastor, the music director, the drama coordinator, and so on). The meeting agenda might appear as follows:

- *A review of last week's service.* Did the service flow well? Did the message, drama or interview, and special music work together in presenting the theme? Is there anything we could have done better? In critiquing the service, always remember that no matter how it went, God's Word never returns empty.
- *A look ahead to next week.* By now the upcoming week's service should be nearly done, with the possible exception of the message from the speaker. Is the chosen music in line with the theme that the pastor will be developing? How about the drama? Any last-minute changes that we need to be aware of?
- *Looking down the road a few weeks.* What's coming up? Are we clear on the theme? Any difficulty in finding music to fit the theme? Have we decided on who we will be interviewing? How is the drama coming along?

- *Taking the long look*. Do a quick review of the next few months' themes to clarify the direction of upcoming worship services.

Step 5: Huddle between services. In cases where the church offers multiple services, the worship team may want to huddle between the services for any last-minute "tweaking." Perhaps the song used before the message will fit better before the drama. Maybe the drama didn't work and needs to be dropped. A strong, committed worship team is not afraid to fix what didn't work at the first service even if it means that the worship bulletin will not be correct at the second.

Effective worship services take consistent planning and work. That planning and work will certainly be rewarding as people encounter God in a relevant way. And that planning will be fun and energizing when it's done as a team.

Don't Be Afraid of Drama

TEREY SUMMERS

Sunk down in the theater seat, with half a bag of popcorn in my lap, eyes fixed on the larger-than-life screen, I find myself bawling my eyes out! Me, and about 150 other people in the movie theater!

In the relative privacy of a friend's living room I am bent over, gasping for air, my face as red as a vine-ripened tomato and my mouth agape. I let out a wave of roaring laughter that puts my bladder to the test! I pause the VCR to catch my breath. I should know better! My old tape of *I Love Lucy* reruns always does that to me.

Whether it's laughter or tears, or anything in between, there's no doubt about it: The art of drama is a powerful thing! Drama touches us in ways nothing else can. Our inhibitions fall away. Suddenly, it doesn't matter that we are

with 150 people we don't know who are crying. We don't mind being overtaken with laughter in a friend's living room. We've been touched.

So why use drama in your worship service or at a church function? I've already answered that question, but generally, when we show up on Sunday morning or Saturday night we are guarding something. Perhaps we arrive willingly, but not necessarily with an open heart. After taking a beating from a long work week, we are not ready to let down the wall that pro- tects our emo-

tions. Fair enough! But drama has a way of getting through the wall. And if not through it, then over, around, or under it. Drama not only communicates a message, it also prepares a person to be a more open "receiver" of messages to follow.

I am a professional actress. I lived and worked for nine years in the Los Angeles/Hollywood area. I still work in every aspect of dramatic performance. From film to stage, radio and television, this business is part of me. While raised in a Christian home and attending church regularly, I wanted an outlet in the church for my talents and gifts.

But, where do I use drama at church? Of course, the more familiar places include your seasonal celebrations, such as Christmas musicals or Easter and Palm Sunday productions. Certainly these productions inspire church members. These dramas can also help attract unchurched persons, or those who are nominally members of the church, such that they only appear during major holy days. If the main purpose of the Sunday service is to appeal to unchurched persons, then you want to make regular use of drama in the service.

To get started, you can investigate any of the following drama resources:

- Willow Creek Community Church in South Barrington, Illinois publishes their dramas (*Willow Creek Resources*, Zondervan).
- Lillenas Publishing Company has a great selection. Not everything will wow you, but there's a good variety of dramas from which to choose.
- *Acting on Faith: Worship Plays from the*

Covenant Players by Charles M. Tanner (Abingdon Press, 1994).
- Terey Summer's church drama skits (For a catalogue, see the address below.)

By writing your own dramatic skits, you unleash amazing creativity and enthusiasm for faith sharing. Few churches have someone on staff to do this, but there are volunteers who are seeking such a creative outlet. Each congregation has the capability of developing its own original material. Even if done only occasionally, customized dramatic material can be a powerful outreach tool.

The drama team needs advance notice from the pastor on topics and scripture passages for any service or function. The elements of putting original scripts together, though not necessarily easy to master, are rather basic and are derived from storytelling.

The structure of drama skits should be consistent: (1) colorful characters; (2) a location or setting; (3) a conflict or angst; and (4) a resolution using the principle message topic.

Most skits work best when set as a parallel situation, rather than a replay of a scriptural narrative. But you must be the judge of what may communicate best to your congregation in any given drama. (See the multivolume series, *The Storyteller's Companion to the Bible,* edited by Michael Williams and Dennis Smith, Abingdon Press, 1990, for suggestions and tips on developing parallel situations or biblical texts into dramatic retellings.)

I write most skits with a heavy comedic hand. I know that laughter is effective in a worship service. Some persons with emotions in check may feel that laughter does not belong within worship, but I contend that *laughter is God's medicine*. It breaks down specific barriers, and the actual physical benefits of laughter have been thoroughly studied! Laughter allows us to be vulnerable if even for a moment. But in that moment God can use the message of a pastor, or a solo, to penetrate a heart that otherwise has closed its valves to block God's presence. Don't be afraid to laugh on Sunday morning! From time to time God also has a good laugh at us on Sunday mornings!

Another form of drama is the Reader's Theater. Reader's Theater is a much more subdued and unobtrusive medium of drama. It's very simply staged, on a stool or at a music stand or podium, and memorization isn't even necessary because the script, to state the obvious, is read (which is great for beginning actors). You can also break up scripture into two or three sections that could develop into a dialogue, back and forth between actors (a way to write your own Reader's Theater).

If you're beginning a drama ministry at your church, and you're looking for actors, put an ad in your bulletin or church paper. Theater folk love a place to ham it up! If there is a slim response, don't worry. Start small. Keep things simple, while at the same time make them great. You can always polish "simple" so that it will shine! But "elaborate" can, and most often will, unravel on you if you don't have much experience. Keeping things simple calls for more imagi-

native participation from your audience—and that's the intent.

Once you have a core group of actors together, evaluate their strengths and appoint someone to the helm (if you don't have a paid staff person in charge). This person doesn't need a master's degree in theater, but should be willing to work and organize the group. Set up regular meetings for brainstorming, perhaps for writing custom dramas, and for rehearsals.

You may be asking, "What if I don't have trained professional actors to work with?" Count it a blessing! I have found that people coming to the "drama" ministry with little or no experience have less work to do in clearing the "dramatics of thea-et-a" out of the way. The "thea-et-a" experts who say, "this is how you do it," often get in the way of being a true vessel that God can use.

Know your actors, know their strengths and weaknesses, and cast them accordingly. Don't overchallenge them unnecessarily, especially if they aren't as strong as some others may be. Natural ability is much more convincing in the congregation than "trained" actors.

Terey Summers is the drama director at Community Church of Joy in Glendale, Arizona. She works professionally on screen and stage and has been named Arizona Actress of the Year. Terey also offers workshops for congregations interested in starting a drama ministry. For more information or for a catalogue of Terey's scripts, please write to: Sherry Summers (Terey's Mama), 1316 West Mountain Sky Ave., Phoenix, AZ 85015.

How to Conduct Interviews During Worship

TIM WRIGHT

Real-life faith stories, when properly used, can add inspiration and content to the worship experience. These testimonies enable people to see the gospel in action. Stories help make the gospel real and accessible by putting "flesh" on it. They remove barriers of the faith that may confuse newcomers by making the gospel personal and understandable. One can always argue about abstract Christian doctrine and theological concepts. But stories of God's grace are hard to dismiss. Stories carry with them the power to move a message from the mind to the heart!

Many congregations use testimonies with varying degrees of success. A well-presented faith story can equal the impact of a month of messages. On the other hand, a poorly presented testimony—one lacking enthusiasm, coherency, or brevity—can drag on like a month of sermons. I have found that the use of interviews takes advantage of the positive aspects of testimonies while helping to eliminate some of the negatives.

An interview format is familiar to many unchurched persons who have watched hundreds of hours of talk show interviews. The interview allows the pastor or worship leader to guide the testimony and keep it focused. Through well-chosen questions the interviewer can "pull out" of the interview the specific information he or she feels would be most helpful and inspirational. The interview format also helps take the pressure off those being interviewed. They realize that they're not alone. Someone will be there to guide them through the conversation.

The following suggestions can help make interviews effective:

1. Choose a good interviewer. The person leading the interview is as important as the person being interviewed. He or she can make or break the interview. The interviewer should be articulate. She or he should be able to ask the right questions—questions that get to the heart of the story. The interviewer should also be quick on her or his feet. Sometimes an answer may prompt a whole new line of questioning that the interviewer didn't expect. He or she needs to be able to listen and formulate new questions as needed.

The interviewer should also be a person who inspires confidence in the person being interviewed. Part of the interviewer's job is to help the interviewee relax and feel comfortable. If the interviewer is nervous, he or she will make the interviewee nervous.

Finally, the interviewer should have a sense of humor. Humor breaks down walls and opens people up to the message. Being quick with a funny comment or question makes for a more personal, enjoyable interview. I find that the interviews containing humor ultimately have the most impact. The audience is so relaxed by the give-and-take they see on the stage that when the message of Christ is presented they are open and ready to hear it.

Choosing the right interviewer is vitally important. This person may or may not be the pastor. Use someone who is competent on stage and also good at drawing out people.

2. Choose a good interviewee. A good story doesn't always equal a good interview. Some people simply do not have the necessary communication skills to tell their story in front of an audience. When looking for a good interview, look not only for a strong story, but also for an articulate, well-spoken person. Seek out people who are adequately comfortable in front of an audience. I've been through seven-minute interviews that lasted an eternity because the person wasn't gifted in public speaking. (This is another reason you need a good interviewer—to cover for a squeamish interviewee!)

Interviewees can be found in all kinds of places. Every congregation has people with stories to tell. Perhaps someone weathered a personal crisis and can talk about how faith and the congregation helped her or him through it. Maybe someone became a believer through the ministry of the church. Perhaps a couple can be interviewed on how they are building a strong, dynamic marriage. Maybe a single parent can share some of the unique challenges she or he faces and how the church can be a support. Some communities have pro, semi-pro, or college teams with Christian athletes who might be willing to come and share their stories. At our congregation we offer to make a donation to the public figure's favorite charity in appreciation for their time with us. Business people, newscasters, radio personalities, and so on also make for great interviews.

3. Use a good introduction. The introduction sets up the interview and its purpose. It gives insight into what the interviewee will be talking about. For example, "This morning we are delighted to have Mike Smith with us. Mike has an incredible story to tell about how God saved his life. Please welcome Mike as he comes to share with us today," or "Today I'm excited to introduce to you a very special guest who is going to talk about life in the NFL. Would you please welcome. . . ." Simply saying, "Here's Carol!" doesn't quite cut it.

4. Have some fun. Create an atmosphere in the interview that allows the interviewee and the audience to relax—an atmosphere that will open the hearts of the audience to what the interviewee has to share.

When I do interviews I like to begin with a few "fun" questions. Essentially I'm having a conversation with the interviewee, and the audience gets to listen in. Starting out with "light" questions draws people into the interview and makes the interviewee more human. For example, I once asked a former player with the Canadian Football League about his most embarrassing play. He told of an incident when, at the end of the game, he ran off the field and accidentally knocked down a "little old lady." He helped her back up, profusely apologizing as he did. Once she was up she said, "It's OK, son. I was watching you play today. And that was the best hit you made all day."

In another interview I asked Ron Wolfley, then with the Cleveland Browns football team, about any plays that stood out in his mind from his career. He shared a story about a Monday night game in Chicago. His assignment was to block William "the Refrigerator" Perry. "The Fridge" weighed well over three hundred pounds. On one crucial play William Perry fell on top of Ron Wolfley. Ron said that at first he thought he had blacked out because Perry's body completely enveloped him. Ron couldn't see a thing. In speaking of Perry he said, "When you weigh almost four hundred pounds, you have stuff hangin' on you don't even know you have!"

Whether it's a humorous story or a bit of personal information about the interviewee, these light questions help people "tune in" to the interview and help put the interviewee at ease.

5. Choose good questions. The interviewer should know the interviewee well enough to ask the right questions—questions that will get to the essence and power of the story. As just stated, depending on the interviewee and his or her testimony, I often begin with a few light questions in order to ease into the heart of the story. For example, "How long have you been attending our congregation, and how did you find us?" or "When did you and Chris first meet?" and so on. Sometimes the story itself is so powerful that the interviewer may want to get right at it. "I understand that four months ago the doctors told your family that you wouldn't survive the night. Tell us about it." I almost always know exactly what four or five questions I want to ask before getting up on stage. Those questions may change during the interview, but I want to be as prepared as possible.

Sometimes, for the sake of time and clarity, the interviewer can set up a question by filling in some of the blanks. "I understand that you were in a car accident involving four cars. Your car was completely totaled and the police say it was a miracle that you walked away alive let alone unharmed. That experience had to change your life. What did you learn from it?"

6. Give the interviewee a general idea of the questions, but don't get too specific. Part of the charm of an interview is its spontaneity. If the interviewee comes too prepared, he or she may appear "canned" or rehearsed. On a couple of occasions I overprepped the interviewees by telling them the specific questions I planned on asking. At the beginning of the interview, when I asked them the first question they, because of nervousness, proceeded to talk for six minutes answering all the questions I wanted to ask before I had a chance to ask them. It was a speech rather than a conversation.

7. Keep control of the microphone. The interviewer should keep control of the interview as much as possible for the sake of time. So I like to hold the mike for the interviewee under her or his chin.

8. Keep the interview to five to ten minutes. Any longer than that and people start to tune out, unless it's an exceptionally powerful story.

9. Get to the heart of the message. The point of an interview is to hear how Jesus Christ can make a difference in life. Telling the story of faith is what the interview is all about.

The first time I used an interview was in 1988 when our congregation launched its "seeker" service. The St. Louis Cardinals had just moved to Phoenix. Ron Wolfley, then a special teams pro-bowler with the team (before he joined Cleveland) agreed to be interviewed during our first service. Before the interview I told him I would ask him a few questions about his career and family. Since he was used to being interviewed I didn't need to give him specific questions—with one exception. I did tell him that at one point I would ask him something like this: "Ron, you're a pro-bowl football player. You have a lot of notoriety, people cheer you from the stands, and you no doubt do OK financially. You have it all. So why does a person like you need Jesus Christ?" At that point, I told him, he was free to share whatever he wanted to about his faith in Jesus.

Ron was a delightful interview. He was quick, funny, and articulate. And when I asked him why he needed Jesus Christ, he simply and powerfully said, "What does it profit a man to gain the whole world and lose his soul?" He then went on to briefly talk about the security and joy Jesus provided him in his life. When seekers hear a football star talk about Jesus, they receive quite an impact!

Of course, athletes, heroes, and "personalities" aren't the only credible interviews. The possibilities are limitless as we look into our congregation and community for stories of faith that inspire and invite us to consider the good news of Jesus.

Preaching to the Unchurched

DOUG MURREN

You're not a preacher are you?" the young man slurred at me from his aisle seat. We were both flying to Denver. He had finally asked my vocation.

I replied to my new friend, "No, I am more like a talker or question answerer."

"You mean like a talk show host or something?" he replied. I couldn't detect whether he was being insulting or not.

"Well, more like a talk show host who tries to speak to a heart, rather than an audience," I said, as I felt my explanations running out.

"Cool. I can see that—you say you do rock and country stuff for music?" He was becoming discernibly enthused. "I'd go to a God show like that!"

I grimaced from the mental picture he'd just painted for me. But his picture did serve an important purpose. It reminded me of the treacherous nature of the word *preach*.

Getting to Know Your Audience

The first principle for preaching to the unchurched is to admit that: *The unchurched don't want to be preached at.* They want to enter into a dialogue, a conversation with your ideas and their own ideas. Does this mean we should all employ a question/answer mode of communicating? No, I think not. However, you'd be surprised at how effective real questioning can be when you move the pulpit aside, periodically, and become vulnerable to the audience.

By dialogue I mean a style that begins with efforts to hear the pain, challenges, and joys of our listeners, especially the unchurched guests in our midst. How can you listen before you preach? Here are a few quantifiable ways:

1. Read magazines. Read *American Demographics, People,* or *Interviews* before you choose your text. Bring the Bible to bear on issues very present in the lives of the unconvinced, and "they will come."

2. Take surveys. Conduct surveys of the community within a five-mile radius of your church. You can hire someone to do these for a reasonable price, but it is much more fun and instructive to do them yourself. Ask questions like:

- What do you like least about church?
- Do you believe God is for you or against you? Why?
- What are the greatest issues you are facing in your life?
- What would be the most pleasant surprise to you if you ever returned to church?

3. Conduct a demographic analysis. Study the demographics of your community to begin to know who you need to reach—their age groups and life situations. What you discover may alter your understanding of what a "perfect" sermon is for your location.

A few years ago I was doing a follow-up analysis of our community's profile from the census bureau data. I discovered that there were ten thousand single mothers within three miles around our church. This awareness has really affected our messages for quite a while.

4. Meet the people. Meet and get to know the people of your community and then prepare your sermons based on how and what you want to say to them. I have always found that preparing a message for one person works better in tone and focus.

Communication today is like competing in one of the prairie rushes for land in the last century. Everything influences everything else in a sophisticated and overstuffed communication arena. We are affected, and we, too, must race to stake our claim.

The Postmodern Grid

Your knowledge of the grid that people use to filter messages is essential to good communication. Postmodern culture has a worldview that should not be overlooked. This worldview is the grid through which persons evaluate messages.

Here is an outline of the postmodern listening grid:

Hyper-individualistic: "I am the final decider of all truth, right and wrong."

Non-belongers: "There is nothing about me that should respond to anyone else's belief systems."

Relativistic: "Right and wrong depends on the situation and person. There is no absolute truth, just covenant truth or romantic truth."

No concept of ultimate authority: "Why should I listen to the Bible more than the Maharishi? One truth is just as good as another. In fact, it is immoral to say you speak for God."

Skeptical/Cynical: "I know what all those preachers are really like."

Time-starved: "I don't really have time to listen to church stuff. My kids are all in Little League and dance. And Harry has to travel three days a week."

Extremely lonely: "I don't know anyone at that church. I wish I did."

Depressed: "I just don't ever really feel good enough to be a church person."

Confused: "I hear so many different things about God and religion, I don't know what's true. Jim is into Islam and Tim and Janice go in for the meditation stuff. It all just overwhelms me."

Irrational: "I like to just go by my feelings. And I am usually a very wonderful person. I don't need much more help."

This is the grid you are speaking through to truly church-inexperienced people. These people hate one other word more than *preaching,* and that's the word *unchurched.* Our evangelism jargon makes them feel like they showed up without their trousers.

Environmental Factors

Church-inexperienced people are also more attuned to the environment of communication than churched folks. What do I mean by environment? Here are a few environmental factors:

The lighting. Listening to "Pastor Raccoon" is adequate for churched people, not for the inexperienced.

The mood of the people. They are sensitive to the mood being conveyed, and if it is uptight, they sneak out during announcements.

How welcomed they feel. Nothing can be done about this from the podium. Only a spiritually gifted layperson can help welcome inexperienced persons.

The spiritual traits that the congregation exudes. Warmth is best. Fear of doing wrong is less entreating. A mission to straighten out everyone is lost on this one.

Excellence. Christians will put up with Sister Martha's wrong chords on the piano; Mr. and Mrs. Inexperienced will not.

Do they sense there are others like them? They can tell when others around them are learning and growing.

Being a competent controller of the environment is the first step in reaching the unchurched. A message can be handicapped by its physical, emotional, and spiritual surroundings.

The amount of time spent on these factors must be equal to that which is spent on the textual analysis and preparation for the sermon. Church-inexperienced people today thrive on love, acceptance, and forgiveness. This kind of environment is addicting, attracting, and transforming.

Other Considerations

The greatest treasure for an inexperienced listener is a concept too often lacking in church: Fun. Is your service fun? Do people laugh? Is the music ever fun? Not trite, but fun?

Inexperienced people have too many problems and concerns to hear more of them. Their condition demands the kind of faith that lightens the day. And they soak up hope like a cactus drinks desert rain. The longing for hope is the number one reason why the unchurched try church in the first place.

And finally, preaching to the unchurched requires identifying with their shame. The unchurched listeners seek forgiveness and need a compassionate pastor to risk association with them in their guilt and shame.

A dissertation on confession and repentance—as essential an ingredient as it is to salvation—won't be heard until it is seen in terms of flesh-and-blood human beings. The inexperienced today want to watch someone else in their forgiveness and repentance to see how genuine it is.

Broken people take time to recognize their own faith. And today, the preconversion phase while attending church can be as long as one to three years. Why so long? I believe it takes this long to get their communication filters adjusted. As they watch the church's progress to wholeness, modeling honesty and forgiveness in its behavior, they, too, are motivated to try the path to personal forgiveness and wholeness. Preaching that reaches the unchurched requires honesty, vulnerability, and a sense of progression along that path to wholeness.

When I gave a sermon on joy for those who couldn't experience it through what they are facing, I briefly shared one of my lifelong medical challenges. I suffer from manic-depression and am regulated with medication. I wasn't sure what the reception would be. But I was overwhelmed and humbled when I saw the response.

We have approximately 350 people seeking help from one of our Twelve Step groups, our counseling clinic, and through pastoral prayer. Most said, "If Doug can show us where he hurts, then I know I don't have to be perfect either." The response continues. At least ten to twenty people a month, quite a number not yet reborn of the Spirit, meet me and say, "My faith grew stronger when I heard your pain."

Reaching forth and delivering a message to the unchurched requires deliberate awareness and self-effacing evaluation, but it is so rewarding and so much fun to reach the empty-hearted that it's worth the struggle.

For the unchurched, like that young businessman on the airplane, who tune in to my "God show" with cynical misgivings, I do what I can to see that they come away with a new way of thinking about what it is to have church be a part of their lives.

Doug Murren is the president of Square One Ministries in Redmond, WA. He is a speaker, author, evangelist, and coach, who leads workshops for pastors and congregations. He is the author of *The Baby Boomerang* and *Leadershift*, both published by Regal/Gospel Light Books.

Characteristics of Seeker-Sensitive Prayers

TIM WRIGHT

Congregations eager to reach out to new people through worship look at every aspect of the service through the eyes of a first-time guest. While worship planners immediately focus on how music and sermons will be affected by such a perspective, one aspect of worship often not considered is the time of public prayer.

Prayer is a hot topic in our country today. Part of the current interest in spirituality can be linked to a renewed interest in prayer. Congregations across the country are jump-starting or beginning prayer ministries. Several churches have hired full-time pastors of prayer. But the interest in prayer isn't limited only to Christians. Non-Christians and "nonreligious" people are also tuning in to prayer. As a result, several major news magazines have devoted cover stories to this "new" phenomenon. So seekers bring some kind of comprehension of prayer. But public prayer, because of its highly religious nature, can lose seekers if we don't keep them in mind. Theological words, long pauses for silence, assumed responses ("Lord, in your mercy," "Hear our prayer"), too many "inside" requests, and an impersonal tone can turn off someone's delicate interest in the power and promise of prayer.

A look at the following characteristics of seeker-sensitive prayers can help congregations better involve unchurched persons during times of prayer.

Seeker-sensitive prayers are:

1. Informal. Rather than formal, written prayers, seeker-sensitive prayers come from the heart of the person leading the prayer. In a sense, seeker-sensitive prayers flow spontaneously out of the moment. This flow does not mean that the prayer is contrived or irrational. Each prayer may have a specific focus to it. It may be an opening prayer, thanking God for his presence. It may be a prayer of confession, asking God for forgiveness. But instead of being written out and read, which gives prayer a formal, literary feel, the prayer is offered informally and usually without notes. If written, the speaker writes the prayer as he or she would speak it, by writing for the ear, not the eye.

2. Intimate. Most formalized, written prayers elicit awe. Seeker-sensitive prayers focus on intimacy. They speak personally to God and often focus more on Jesus. Instead of addressing a far-off dignitary with royal language, seeker-sensitive prayers address a God who is present here and now, a God who is accessible. Thou's and Thee's are not allowed.

3. Conversational. Rather than using religious jargon, seeker-sensitive prayers use common language in addressing God. Such prayers sound like a conversation between two people rather than a speech being recited.

4. Focused. Most formal, written prayers tend to be rather long. Many services end with a significant prayer time that includes praying for many needs locally, nationally, and internationally. Seekers are unable to concentrate for long periods of time in corporate prayer. So seeker-sensitive prayers stay focused on a specific subject and tend to be brief. Rather than one long prayer, seeker-sensitive services use several brief prayers.

Examples

The following prayers are examples of seeker-sensitive prayers. These prayers are not meant to be used in services. When a prayer sounds canned or read, seekers tune it out.

God,

Thanks for the chance we have to worship you today. We ask that through the music, the drama, and the message, you would speak to us and teach us something new about your love for us. In Jesus' name, Amen.

Gracious God,

We admit to you today that we have not been all that we should be. We've failed you, ourselves, and others. We ask that you would set us free from anything and everything that keeps us from enjoying you, including our failures, our hurts, and our disappointments. Thanks for caring enough about us to meet our every need. In Jesus' name, Amen.

Jesus,

We ask that as we take a few minutes to look at this story about you that you would quiet our hearts and help us to listen. We look forward to all you have for us today. Amen.

Forgiving Father,

We thank you for this opportunity to take a few moments to bring some of our concerns to you. Thank you for hearing and responding with our best in mind. We pray for (a few brief requests can be made at this point). We take some time now to share with you our own needs and concerns in this moment of silence. (Having some soft music playing underneath helps warm up the atmosphere and removes the uncomfortable feeling many may have sitting in silence.) Again, God, thanks for hearing our prayers and for promising to take care of us. In Jesus' name we pray, Amen.

Tips on Staging
TIM WRIGHT

Staging for a contemporary outreach-oriented service can pose an interesting problem for churches designed for traditional worship. By its very nature contemporary worship takes on a "performance" feel. The singers, the praise band, and the drama actors will want to be front and center as much as possible. But in most denominational churches, the stage is already filled with an altar, choir loft, baptismal font, pulpit, lectern, and chairs for the worship leaders. And most of those pieces are not movable. So where do you put a contemporary band?

1. Front and Center Stage. If the chancel furniture is not movable, and the platform area is small, the band may need to set up on the side of the stage. But the singers and the actors (if drama is used) should be in the center of the stage if possible, or at least on the stage but off to one side. Those born after 1946 were raised on rock concerts in which the band and singers performed from center stage. A contemporary service works better if that feel is accepted.

If the altar furniture is immovable but the stage area is large enough, you may want to set the band up in front of the furniture. In some congregations this may border on sacrilege, but again, putting the group center stage gives the band/singers an unstated authority as worship leaders.

Another option might be to put the band and singers on the floor directly in front of the altar area. Some churches may find it necessary to remove a front pew or two in order to fit in the group. It may be that putting the whole group off to one side may be the only option available. The point is to create the sense that the band is a viable part of the worship experience.

2. Remove the Furniture. If the altar furniture is movable, move it! At our church we use the altar furniture at our first two services but move it out for the others. This frees up stage space for the band, singers, and actors. It also cleans up the stage and creates a concert atmosphere.

The key in staging is to ensure that people can see the action and that the stage is as free from clutter and overcrowding as possible.

3. Move the Service. Another staging option is to move the service to a fellowship hall or gymnasium where the stage can be devoted to the band without interfering with the traditional worship space.

We experiment continually with the look of the stage. If it doesn't work one week, we'll change it the next. We may use a particular staging configuration for a few months and then make some changes to add variety. However, throughout all the different staging options we've tried, I still find the one that communicates the best is the one that puts the band, singers, and actors front and center stage. It focuses people's attention up front and creates an atmosphere of energy and excitement.

Resource Kit 3

SEEKER SERVICES

Notes: This kit includes *two sample services* and *two sample messages*. It also offers *a Christmas Eve service/message* and *an Easter service/message*. In addition, *sample dramas are provided.*

   The worship choruses listed in the services can be found in the chart in Resource Kit #2. Choruses in that chart marked by ** would be appropriate for outreach-oriented seeker services. For communion choruses, you may want to choose more worshipful songs.

   This kit also includes two performance music charts. The first chart lists songs that can be found on recordings and in music books. The second chart lists songs for which printed music is unavailable as of this printing. To use these songs you will want to find someone with the ability to "lift" the song off a recording to produce a chart for the band. The vocal parts will have to be pulled off the recording as well.

   The themes used in the charts are intentionally broad. Many of the songs will fit several different topics.

Key for Styles

P = pop	S = slow tempo
R = rock	M = moderate tempo
C = country	F = fast tempo
J = jazz	MS = moderately slow tempo
PR = pop/rock	MF = moderately fast tempo
CP = country/pop	

SEEKER COMMUNION SERVICE
Sermon Series
How to Build Healthy Relationships—
PART ONE

How to Build Healthy Relationships

MARK 1:40-42

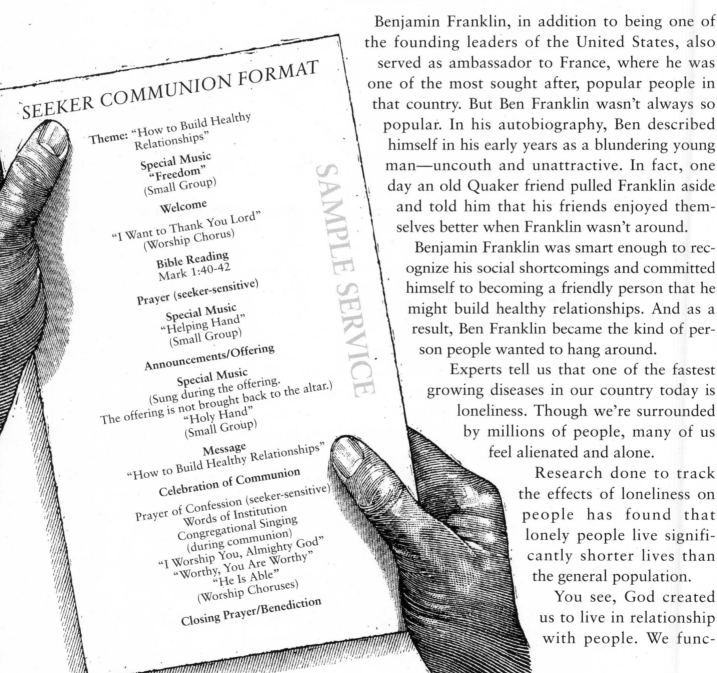

SEEKER COMMUNION FORMAT

SAMPLE SERVICE

Theme: "How to Build Healthy Relationships"

Special Music
"Freedom"
(Small Group)

Welcome

"I Want to Thank You Lord"
(Worship Chorus)

Bible Reading
Mark 1:40-42

Prayer (seeker-sensitive)

Special Music
"Helping Hand"
(Small Group)

Announcements/Offering

Special Music
(Sung during the offering.
The offering is not brought back to the altar.)
"Holy Hand"
(Small Group)

Message
"How to Build Healthy Relationships"

Celebration of Communion

Prayer of Confession (seeker-sensitive)
Words of Institution
Congregational Singing
(during communion)
"I Worship You, Almighty God"
"Worthy, You Are Worthy"
"He Is Able"
(Worship Choruses)

Closing Prayer/Benediction

Benjamin Franklin, in addition to being one of the founding leaders of the United States, also served as ambassador to France, where he was one of the most sought after, popular people in that country. But Ben Franklin wasn't always so popular. In his autobiography, Ben described himself in his early years as a blundering young man—uncouth and unattractive. In fact, one day an old Quaker friend pulled Franklin aside and told him that his friends enjoyed themselves better when Franklin wasn't around.

Benjamin Franklin was smart enough to recognize his social shortcomings and committed himself to becoming a friendly person that he might build healthy relationships. And as a result, Ben Franklin became the kind of person people wanted to hang around.

Experts tell us that one of the fastest growing diseases in our country today is loneliness. Though we're surrounded by millions of people, many of us feel alienated and alone.

Research done to track the effects of loneliness on people has found that lonely people live significantly shorter lives than the general population.

You see, God created us to live in relationship with people. We function best, we are at our healthiest, when we have significant, healthy relationships with others.

And yet, many of us are like the young Ben Franklin—we don't have many strong relationships. Some of us find our lives littered with broken, failed relationships and the resulting broken, lonely heart. Others feel that, even though we have friends, we could do a better job at making those friendships stronger and healthier.

Like Ben Franklin, we can develop the habits necessary for building strong, significant, healthy friendships. And the keys to building healthy relationships can be found in the Bible.

In our Bible reading for today we have the true story of a man who desperately needed a friend. Through no fault of his own, this man had been ostracized from society. He was an outcast because he had the misfortune of being stricken with leprosy, a skin disease that caused as much fear then as HIV/AIDS does today. Because people feared catching leprosy, lepers were forced to live outside the city. They were forbidden any kind of contact with healthy people. People threw rocks at lepers to keep them at a distance. Should people come their way, lepers were required to warn them by yelling, "Unclean! Unclean!" Imagine what that did to a leper's self-esteem.

For the man in our story, the alienation and loneliness had to be overwhelming. He was a person who needed a friend. And one day, a friend came into his life.

The leper learned that Jesus was nearby, so he sought Jesus out, hoping for a miracle. And in his encounter with Jesus he not only received the healing he wanted, but he also found a friend—one who loved and accepted him unconditionally.

This morning we're going to take a deeper look at this story. For in looking at Jesus' response to the leper we can find some important keys for building healthy relationships. And in the process, it just might be that some of you will meet a new friend—a friend who can transform your life. But before we talk about it, let's pray together.

As we look at the way Jesus responded to the leper we find several principles for building healthy relationships. I'd like to look at some of those principles with you today and if you'd like to take a few notes, I've provided an outline for you in your worship brochure.

First, as we look at the story of Jesus and the leper we see that one of the keys for building healthy relationships is to **decide to see the God-given value in each person.**

While everyone else was repulsed by the leper, Jesus was drawn to him. For Jesus saw beyond the disease to the God-given dignity within him. Jesus always did that. He always decided to see the best in people and to draw the best out of them.

American psychologist and philosopher William James said that the deepest principle in human nature is the craving to be appreciated.

All of us want people to see the best in us, to see and value our God-given worth. People who build strong, healthy relationships continually choose to focus on that God-given worth in others.

During the first day of a speech class the teacher went around the room and asked his students to introduce themselves. They were to respond to two questions: "What do I like about myself?" and "What don't I like about myself?" Hiding in the back of the room was a red-haired girl named Dorothy. Her long hair hung down around her face, almost completely covering it. When it was her turn to answer the questions, the room fell silent. Dorothy refused to say anything. So the teacher moved his chair next to hers and gently repeated the questions.

After another period of silence, Dorothy sighed, sat up in her chair, and pulled back her hair, revealing a large, irregularly shaped, red birthmark on her face. She said, "That should tell you what I don't like about myself."

The teacher was deeply moved by Dorothy's obvious shame and pain and did something he had never done before. He kissed her on the cheek, the cheek with the birthmark, and said, "It's OK, Dorothy, God and I still think you're beautiful."

Dorothy wept uncontrollably for twenty minutes. Not because of the shame, but because she had never experienced that kind of unconditional love before. Few had ever taken the time to affirm her worth and value.

Healthy relationships begin when we choose to see the best in people—when we focus on their God-given value and treat them with dignity.

Second, as we observe the relationship-building skills of Jesus we see that **relationships are strengthened when we learn to listen.**

People didn't hang around to listen to lepers. Instead, they ran away from them as fast as they could. Yet Jesus stopped and listened intently to hear what the leper had to say. He valued the leper enough to hear him out and to then respond to the man's request.

Dale Carnegie said, "You can make more friends in two months by becoming interested in other people than you can in two years by trying to get other people interested in you." In other words, the secret to being interesting is to be interested. And there is no better way to demonstrate true interest than by listening.

The greatest honor that the leper had ever experienced came when Jesus took the time to listen to him. We build healthy relationships when we honor people by listening to them.

A third key for building relationships with people is to **cultivate transparency.**

The Bible says that when he heard and saw the pain of that lonely leper, Jesus was moved with pity. People could actually see in his face and body language that Jesus was deeply concerned about the well-being of the man. His emotions of love and compassion were visible to all. In his dealings with people Jesus was always transparent. He was honest with people. He didn't wear any masks. He didn't try to be someone he wasn't. He was free to express any and all of his emotions.

People are attracted to those who are transparent—to those who are honest and sincere in the way in which they present themselves. As we let people see inside of us we'll find that our relationships become stronger. Transparent people tend to be magnets that attract others.

A fourth key for building healthy relationships is to **demonstrate your affection.**

Not only was Jesus moved with pity at the plight of the leper, but he was also moved with compassion to respond with help. Jesus demonstrated his love in a very tangible way. He reached out and touched the leper.

Here was a man who had had no physical touch from the moment it was learned that he was a leper. Again, people stayed away from him. Fearing they might catch his disease they threw rocks at him to keep him away.

And yet Jesus, overwhelmed with love, reached out and touched the man. And that touch, more than anything else, spoke volumes to that lonely, alienated leper. And through that touch the leper was healed.

Perhaps nothing demonstrates affection more than a meaningful touch. Behavioral research proves over and over again the importance of touch for maintaining health and wholeness.

But more than keeping us healthy, meaningful touch communicates acceptance. By touching the leper Jesus was clearly saying that he wanted to be friends with the man—that he accepted the leper just as he was. A handshake, a hug, holding hands for prayer, a pat on the shoulder, instantly draws two people together like nothing else.

A few years ago a group of medical students were training in the children's ward of a large hospital. One of the students seemed particularly loved by the children. They always greeted him with joy and excitement.

The other medical students wanted to find out why the kids loved this young man so much so they decided to follow him as he made his rounds. They didn't discover anything out of the ordinary until the night rounds. It was then that they observed how he kissed every child good night.

Healthy relationships are built when we demonstrate, in tangible ways, our love and affection for others.

Finally, the last and most important key for building healthy relationships is to **become friends with Jesus.**

In order to make friends we have to be a friend—the kind of person people want to be with. And yet, there are many barriers in life that keep us from being that kind of person.

One of those barriers is a cold heart—a heart that cannot love due to bitterness and anger.

A second barrier is a hurt heart—a heart scarred by failed relationships of the past.

A third barrier is a shy heart—the heart that sees no worth or value in his or her life.

The good news is that just as Jesus brought healing and wholeness to the leper by being his friend, so he can bring healing and wholeness to you by being your friend.

He can thaw your cold heart by removing the bitterness through his unconditional forgiveness and acceptance of you.

He can heal your hurt heart by putting the broken pieces back together.

He can free you from your shy heart by helping you see yourself as he does—as a person with worth and value.

You see, no matter how you feel about yourself, no matter what kind of friend you are right now, Jesus loves you. And he stands ready to shower you with his love just as he did with the leper. He wants to touch you with his compassion. He wants to restore your worth and dignity. He wants to be your lifetime friend, and transform you into the person he created you to be. And as you become friends with Jesus you will find that you are better able to love yourself and others enough to build healthy relationships with them.

So if you're lonely, if your heart is cold, hurt, or shy, I encourage you to let Jesus love you. I invite you to take him up on his offer of friendship. For it's a relationship that will transform your life.

This message was preached at an outreach-oriented service by Tim Wright.

SEEKER SERVICE
Sermon Series

How to Build Healthy Relationships—
PART TWO

How to Resolve Conflict

MATTHEW 18:15-20

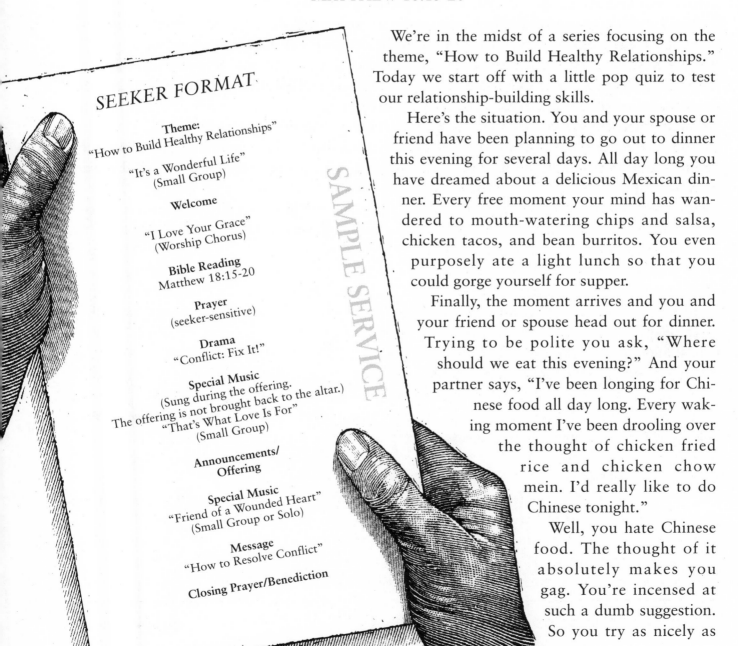

SEEKER FORMAT

Theme:
"How to Build Healthy Relationships"

"It's a Wonderful Life"
(Small Group)

Welcome

"I Love Your Grace"
(Worship Chorus)

Bible Reading
Matthew 18:15-20

Prayer
(seeker-sensitive)

Drama
"Conflict: Fix It!"

Special Music
(Sung during the offering.
The offering is not brought back to the altar.)
"That's What Love Is For"
(Small Group)

Announcements/ Offering

Special Music
"Friend of a Wounded Heart"
(Small Group or Solo)

Message
"How to Resolve Conflict"

Closing Prayer/Benediction

SAMPLE SERVICE

We're in the midst of a series focusing on the theme, "How to Build Healthy Relationships." Today we start off with a little pop quiz to test our relationship-building skills.

Here's the situation. You and your spouse or friend have been planning to go out to dinner this evening for several days. All day long you have dreamed about a delicious Mexican dinner. Every free moment your mind has wandered to mouth-watering chips and salsa, chicken tacos, and bean burritos. You even purposely ate a light lunch so that you could gorge yourself for supper.

Finally, the moment arrives and you and your friend or spouse head out for dinner. Trying to be polite you ask, "Where should we eat this evening?" And your partner says, "I've been longing for Chinese food all day long. Every waking moment I've been drooling over the thought of chicken fried rice and chicken chow mein. I'd really like to do Chinese tonight."

Well, you hate Chinese food. The thought of it absolutely makes you gag. You're incensed at such a dumb suggestion. So you try as nicely as you can to suggest a Mexican meal. You describe your love of hot, spicy food only to notice a sickly look on the face of your friend or spouse. You recall that he or she absolutely hates Mexican food. In fact, your partner gets a rash just from thinking about eating it.

Suddenly, while driving to eat, your relationship hits a snag. So here's the quiz. How do you resolve the conflict? Would you:

A. Go to the Mexican restaurant (because you're driving) and enjoy the meal while your partner suffers?

B. Be a nice person and take your partner to a Chinese restaurant, force down the food, and sulk the entire meal?

C. Drop off your partner at the nearest corner and eat Mexican by yourself?

D. Call a pastor, set up a counseling appointment, and have the pastor help you decide, making sure to choose a pastor who likes Mexican food?

E. Go home and eat leftovers in silence and never speak to your friend or spouse again?

On the surface that conflict seems silly and unimportant. But mismanaged, small, insignificant conflicts grow into unmanageable conflicts.

No relationship, no matter how strong, no matter how deep, is immune to conflict. In fact, the only way to avoid conflict in relationships is to decide to alienate yourself completely from people. Because relationships consist of people with unique personalities, drives, and desires, all relationships run into periods of conflict.

But people in healthy relationships use conflict to their advantage. Rather than seeing conflict as a problem, they view it as an opportunity to strengthen the relationship.

As we continue our series on building healthy relationships, we're going to focus on how to resolve conflict. In the Bible Jesus has some practical, relationship-transforming principles that can not only help us deal effectively with conflict, but that can actually help us grow as individuals and help the relationship grow as well. But before we talk about it, let's pray together.

To resolve conflict we need to begin by understanding what causes conflict. If you'd like to take some notes, I've provided an outline for you in your worship brochure.

One of the most frequent causes of conflict is poor communication—not being clear about what's being asked for or not taking the time to really listen.

A second cause of conflict is unmet needs. When people feel their needs for security or belonging are not being taken seriously, conflict is often the result.

A third cause of conflict is the fear that something of value might be lost—like peace, a friendship, or prosperity.

A fourth cause of conflict is the belief on the part of at least one in the relationship that everything must go his or her way. Self-centeredness can put a lot of strain on a relationship.

In times of conflict, people react in different ways—and some ways are more appropriate than others.

First, some people react to conflict with **aggressiveness.** They believe that their way is the right way. They seek only to satisfy their own concerns at the expense of others and even the relationship. Aggressiveness chooses the Mexican restaurant because that's what I want and I'm driving.

A second response to conflict is **avoidance.** Some people simply ignore the conflict and hope it will go away. They stall, they try to pass the buck, they do anything they can to avoid dealing with the situation. Avoidance goes Chinese and chokes down the food because I don't want to rock the boat.

A third reaction to conflict is **compromise**—working together to come to a win-win solution. Compromise chooses to go to a restaurant we both enjoy and like.

It's that third response to conflict—compromise—that Jesus points us to today in our Bible reading.

In that passage he shares three keys that can help us come to a win-win solution in dealing with conflict, and I'd like to quickly look at those keys with you today.

The first key for coming to a compromise in conflict, according to Jesus, is to seek to **work it out together.**

People in healthy relationships recognize the inevitability of conflict and respond quickly to it by dealing with it together. And there are several steps we can take that can enable us to effectively deal with the conflict before it gets out of hand.

1. The first of those steps is to try to get to the root of the problem. The problem may not be your overwhelming desire for Mexican food. The real issue might be that you're in a job where no one values your opinion. You're always at the mercy of someone else's decisions and for once you would like to make a decision—to do something you want to do.

The real issue may not be the financial strain you're under. It may be a sense of insecurity and loneliness because your spouse is either never home or doesn't pay any attention to you when he or she is home. Getting to the real problem can help us quickly put an end to conflict.

2. A second step for dealing with conflict together is to focus on feelings, not faults. Instead of pointing out your partner's shortcomings, share your emotions. Use "I feel" statements rather than "You are" accusations. If need be, take time out to cool off.

And always watch what you're saying in the heat of the battle. Don't say something you'll later regret. Make a decision that personality bashing is unfair fighting and off-limits.

3. A third step in dealing with conflict together is to focus on solutions, not on blame.

Find a solution that both of you feel good about. Work for a compromise where both of you win.

4. And finally, apologize and forgive freely.

At a dinner party one night Lady Churchill was seated across the table from Sir Winston, who kept making his hand walk up and down on the table—two fingers bent at the knuckles. The fingers appeared to be walking toward Lady Churchill.

Finally, a friend turned to her and asked, "Why is Sir Winston looking at you so wistfully, and whatever is he doing with those two knuckles on the table?"

Lady Churchill replied, "That's simple. We had a mild quarrel before we left home, and he is indicating that it's his fault and he's on his knees to me in abject apology."

Always remember that the relationship is more important than who's right or wrong. People in healthy relationships are quick to apologize and forgive.

So, in seeking compromise in the midst of conflict Jesus encourages us to begin by trying to work out the problem together.

However, sometimes, for whatever reason, two people cannot resolve the conflict together. In those times Jesus encourages us to **seek outside help.** Pastors or professional counselors oftentimes bring a needed third party objective view to the situation. When couples get so involved in the problem, they often miss some of the obvious possibilities. Spending time with a caring third party can help bring a peaceful end to the conflict.

Finally, a third key for bringing about compromise in the midst of conflict is to **surrender your relationship to Jesus Christ.** Jesus makes the promise that where two or three people are gathered in his name, he will be there. He will be there to support the relationship through the storms of conflict. He will be there to put the pieces back together should the conflict cause a tear in the relationship. He will be there to guide and direct us as we seek to resolve the problem. He is the foundation that can make the relationship strong and healthy no matter what the conflict might be.

An actor who at one time had landed many important stage roles now found the jobs drying up. Instinctively, he knew what the problem was. He no longer valued the audience. He felt they were a bunch of jerks. That attitude permeated his performances. The audience could sense it, and soon he was no longer asked to take the important roles.

One day a minister encouraged the actor to pray for the audience before he went on stage. He told the actor to practice love and respect for them. So every night before the performance, the actor stood in the wings and looked out over the audience. He picked out faces and prayed for them. He made a decision to love them. He learned to respect people again, and the audience grew to love and respect him once again.

Surrendering our relationships to Jesus through prayer is the most important step we can take in resolving conflict. For prayer opens us up to his love—a love that holds us, mends the hurts, and sustains the relationship through the struggle. His love and forgiveness enables us to love and forgive one another. Because he treats us with dignity and respect we can treat one another with respect, even in times of disagreement. His love for us can keep our love for one another strong, giving us the will to find win-win solutions to the conflict.

Jesus promises that in the midst of conflict he will be there with you supporting you, encouraging you, and opening you up to solutions to the problem. He is the one who can keep your relationships healthy.

So I invite you today to surrender your life and your relationships to Jesus. His friendship with you will enable you to build better, healthier relationships with others. Let's pray together.

This message was preached at an outreach-oriented service by Tim Wright.

Sample Drama

Conflict: Fix It!

Themes: Relationships
Communication
Marriage
Conflict

Setting: *During a football game, a couple puts their communications skills to the test. The husband is sitting in front of a television set, engrossed in a football game, yelling things like, "Touchdown!" "Twenty yard line!" and so on. The wife does obvious things to try to get his attention. But nothing works.*

Director's Notes: This requires imagination on the part of the audience as well as the actors. The husband has to creatively portray watching television, perhaps using an imaginary remote control, or a real one if necessary. Be sure that both actors have a clear concept of where the "TV" is on stage so that the audience will sense its presence. Outside of this, a chair for the husband to sit in is all that is needed. Be careful that, in the wife's attempt to block the screen, she doesn't keep herself from being seen.

(The wife, after trying to get the husband's attention, finally steps in front of the TV.)

Husband: Honey, could you move. I can't see the TV.

Wife: Oh really. Well, that would be just awful if you had to miss just one second of that football game. I may have to administer CPR. *(Steps in front of the TV again. Husband gasps for air.)*

Husband: (Name), stop, I can't breathe. I need football . . . Someone get me football . . . aaughhh!

Wife: You'll think "need football" when I get done with you. You'll know the power of a linebacker by the time I'm through.

Husband: No, seriously, honey. I'm missing a lot of the game. We haven't talked in a while, and this has been nice . . . *(Pause)* . . . but move!

Wife: I will not move. We have arrived at a bit of a conflict here. This football has become a problem.

Husband: In whose opinion? *(Sees wife's angry look.)* Just kidding.

Wife: I don't think this is funny.

Husband: Neither do I. I'm missing the game.

Wife: Well, you're gonna miss your wife and a couple of kids if we don't resolve this.

Husband: *(Looks as though he's peering through her legs at the game.)*

Wife: Are you ignoring me?

Husband: *(Silence)*

Wife: (Name!) . . . (Name!)

Husband: *(Calmly)* Yes dear?

Wife: You're avoiding this issue.

Husband: Yes, I am dear. You are correct. I am definitely avoiding this particular conflict. Could you please move?!

Wife: Why are you avoiding me? You always do this.

Husband: I always do this when you always do that.

Wife: Do that? Do what? What do I do that makes you do this when I do that?

Husband: Who's on first?

Wife: Stop being funny.

Husband: That's what you do!

Wife: What? What do I do?

Husband: You impose things on me. "Don't be funny!" "Don't watch football!" "It's stupid."

Wife: I don't impose things on you. Yes, football is stupid, mindless, without purpose, irrelevant, and ungodly, but that's my opinion. Well, . . . mine and God's. But that doesn't mean I'm imposing this philosophy on you.

Husband: Oh, yes you are. That's what causes these conflicts between us.

Wife: Oh, so now I'm to blame. I start all of our conflicts. Forget it! Just forget it!!

Husband: Okay, could you move now please?

Wife: I hate conflicts. I hate them, I hate them, I hate them!! They just cause trouble. There's not an ounce of good in them. They're useless.

Husband: *(Of his own free will, turns away from the TV.)* Actually, they aren't completely bad. This little conflict we've had here today has been very informative. I learned something today. Who would have thought football was ungodly?

Wife: Stop it. You're making fun of me.

Husband: Okay, Okay. I'm kidding. But I'm not totally off base here. I did learn a little from our conflict. I learned that when you stand in front of the TV screen, there is still a lot of it I can see.

Wife: *(Looks at him with confusion and disgust.)*

Husband: It's a compliment, I promise. *(Pause)* It's got us talking, anyway. Maybe it's not about who's right or wrong—but conflict definitely makes a statement. If we hadn't had conflict, maybe we wouldn't be talking right now. I don't like having conflicts with you, but I don't think they're anything to run away from. *(Stands up and moves in front of the TV next to his wife.)*

Wife: *(Long pause)* Are you imposing your philosophy on me?

Husband: *(Starts to speak in retort.)* Uh . . .

Wife: Just kidding. Now move, I can't see the TV at all!

SEEKER CHRISTMAS EVE SERVICE

Come Home for the Holidays

LUKE 2:1-21

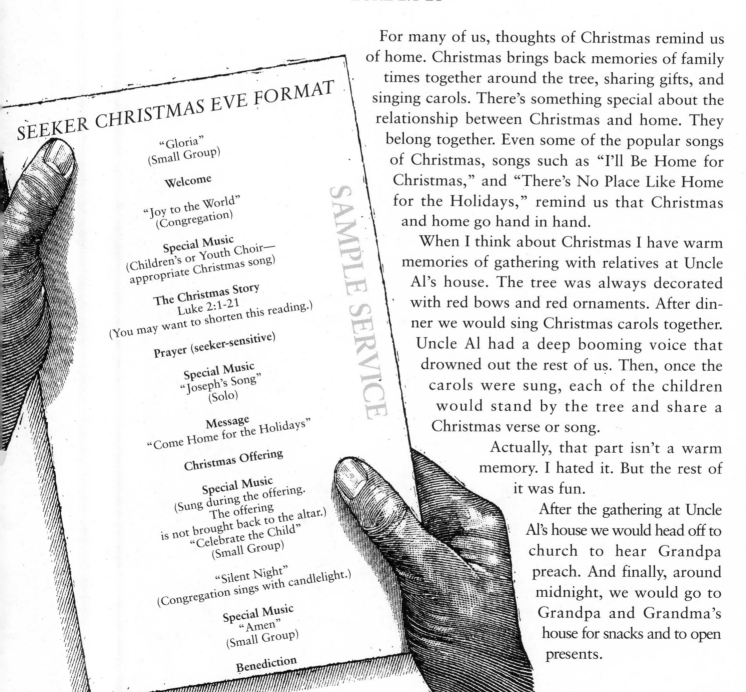

SEEKER CHRISTMAS EVE FORMAT

"Gloria"
(Small Group)

Welcome

"Joy to the World"
(Congregation)

Special Music
(Children's or Youth Choir—
appropriate Christmas song)

The Christmas Story
Luke 2:1-21
(You may want to shorten this reading.)

Prayer (seeker-sensitive)

Special Music
"Joseph's Song"
(Solo)

Message
"Come Home for the Holidays"

Christmas Offering

Special Music
(Sung during the offering.
The offering
is not brought back to the altar.)
"Celebrate the Child"
(Small Group)

"Silent Night"
(Congregation sings with candlelight.)

Special Music
"Amen"
(Small Group)

Benediction

SAMPLE SERVICE

For many of us, thoughts of Christmas remind us of home. Christmas brings back memories of family times together around the tree, sharing gifts, and singing carols. There's something special about the relationship between Christmas and home. They belong together. Even some of the popular songs of Christmas, songs such as "I'll Be Home for Christmas," and "There's No Place Like Home for the Holidays," remind us that Christmas and home go hand in hand.

When I think about Christmas I have warm memories of gathering with relatives at Uncle Al's house. The tree was always decorated with red bows and red ornaments. After dinner we would sing Christmas carols together. Uncle Al had a deep booming voice that drowned out the rest of us. Then, once the carols were sung, each of the children would stand by the tree and share a Christmas verse or song.

Actually, that part isn't a warm memory. I hated it. But the rest of it was fun.

After the gathering at Uncle Al's house we would head off to church to hear Grandpa preach. And finally, around midnight, we would go to Grandpa and Grandma's house for snacks and to open presents.

Christmas is a time when we think about home. We remember the warmth and the love, the compassion and the acceptance, the security and the sense of belonging that home provides.

It's no surprise then that the very first Christmas took place on a journey home. Joseph and Mary, the parents of Jesus, had to travel to the boyhood home of Joseph because of a census being taken at the time. And it was there, in Bethlehem, in Joseph's hometown, that Jesus was born.

Christmas is a time for going home.

And yet for many of us, home isn't what it used to be. Instead of love there's hurt and pain. Instead of harmony and togetherness there's brokenness. Instead of acceptance and security there's alienation and a lack of self-worth. For many, Christmas and home no longer belong together.

The good news of Christmas is that, no matter what's going on in our lives or in our families, we can always come home. There is always a place where we can go and experience love, hope, healing, and security. And that place is found in Jesus Christ.

You see, Christmas is God's invitation to you and to me to come home to him through Jesus. It's his invitation to us to experience his love, his compassion, and his security in an intimate, personal way.

A family was out shopping for their Christmas tree. Dad wanted the perfect tree and was pleased to see so many beautiful trees on the lot. It would be hard to make a decision. After several minutes of browsing, his daughter came running up to him all excited and said, "Daddy, I found the perfect tree." She led him over to it and to his disappointment he saw a small, wilted, almost lifeless tree. He said, "Honey, this tree is pathetic. It's not anywhere near as pretty as the other trees." To which his daughter replied, "I know, Daddy. But I want to take this tree home and make it beautiful."

Through Christmas, God invites us to come home to him that he might love us, care for us, and make us beautiful. He offers us a place where the brokenness can be healed, a place where we can feel safe and secure. He invites us to a place where we can be ourselves and yet grow into the people he created us to be.

Lois Kimberly was a semi-retired teacher living in

New York City. One day she received a call from the principal of a school near her home asking if she would substitute for one of his twelfth-grade classes.

Lois met with the principal and he handed her a list of the students. She looked at the list and noticed a number next to each of the student's names—125, 130, 160, 158, and so on. She said to the principal, "These look like brilliant students. It would be an honor to teach them."

What Lois didn't know was that each of those students had a police record. She was the seventh teacher to work with them that year. So, naively she took the job and was their teacher for the rest of the year. And at the end of the year, every one of those students ended up with an average grade of 3.0.

Lois went on to receive the most valuable teacher award. Though flattered, she said to the principal, "You know there was no way I could lose. My students were brilliant young men and women. There was absolutely no way I could have failed teaching kids with I.Q.'s of 120, 130, and 140. You showed me their I.Q. scores yourself, Mr. Principal."

Puzzled, the principal said, "Lois, I'm not sure what you're talking about. We don't give I.Q. tests in this school."

"But the scores were right next to their names," she said.

The principal was stunned. "Those weren't their I.Q. scores," he said. "Those were their locker numbers."

Those students excelled because Lois believed the best about them and drew the best out of them.

That's what Jesus does for us. When we come home to him he accepts us just as we are and then loves us into the people he created us to be. He sees past our failures and shortcomings to the possibilities created in us. He restores our dignity. When we come home to Jesus we find a love that unlocks a new sense of worth and value.

Wilbur and Orville Wright had tried repeatedly to fly a heavier-than-air aircraft without success. Finally, one December day, off the sand dunes of Kitty Hawk, they did what humans had never done before. They flew. Elated, they wired their sister Katherine. The telegram said, "We have actually flown 120 feet. Will be home for Christmas."

Upon receiving the telegram, Katherine raced down the street to the city editor of the local newspaper to show him the scoop of the century. He read the message carefully and said, "Well, how nice. The boys will be home for Christmas."

There's nothing more important than being home for the holidays. And no matter who you are, no matter what your home is like, you can come home once and for all to God. For Christmas is God's invitation to you to come home to his peace, his love, and his security. It's his invitation to you to live in a relationship with him so that Christmas might happen in you each and every day.

And the way to come home for the holidays is to welcome the Christ of Christmas, Jesus, into your life. Jesus came to bring us home, to make it possible for us to live in a personal relationship with God.

So I encourage you this Christmas Eve to take God up on this invitation to come home by receiving Jesus into your life. Come home to God's love and care. Come home to a place of acceptance and compassion. It's the place you've been longing for. It's the place that can transform your life. Let's pray together.

This message was preached at an outreach-oriented Christmas Eve service by Tim Wright.

SEEKER EASTER SERVICE

What We'll Do for Love

ROMANS 5:6-8

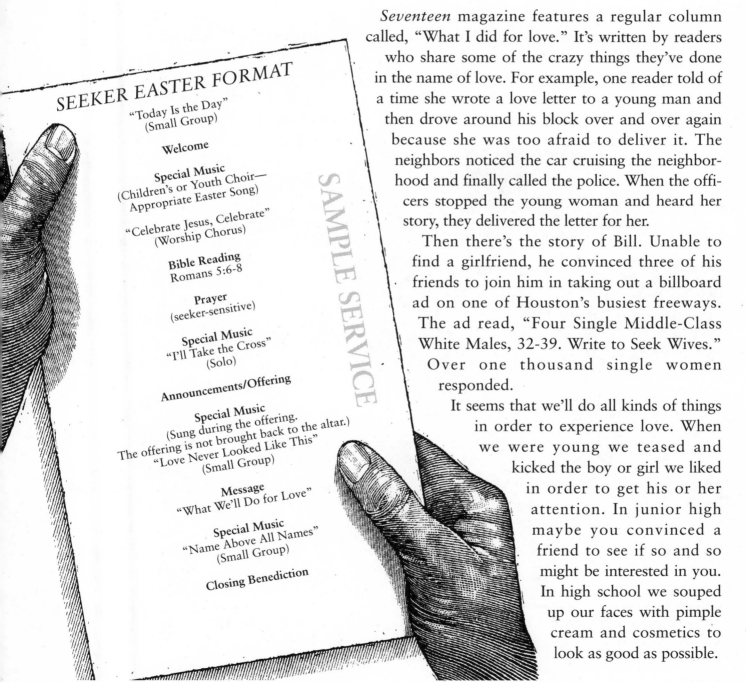

SEEKER EASTER FORMAT

"Today Is the Day"
(Small Group)

Welcome

Special Music
(Children's or Youth Choir—
Appropriate Easter Song)

"Celebrate Jesus, Celebrate"
(Worship Chorus)

Bible Reading
Romans 5:6-8

Prayer
(seeker-sensitive)

Special Music
"I'll Take the Cross"
(Solo)

Announcements/Offering

Special Music
(Sung during the offering.
The offering is not brought back to the altar.)
"Love Never Looked Like This"
(Small Group)

Message
"What We'll Do for Love"

Special Music
"Name Above All Names"
(Small Group)

Closing Benediction

SAMPLE SERVICE

Seventeen magazine features a regular column called, "What I did for love." It's written by readers who share some of the crazy things they've done in the name of love. For example, one reader told of a time she wrote a love letter to a young man and then drove around his block over and over again because she was too afraid to deliver it. The neighbors noticed the car cruising the neighborhood and finally called the police. When the officers stopped the young woman and heard her story, they delivered the letter for her.

Then there's the story of Bill. Unable to find a girlfriend, he convinced three of his friends to join him in taking out a billboard ad on one of Houston's busiest freeways. The ad read, "Four Single Middle-Class White Males, 32-39. Write to Seek Wives." Over one thousand single women responded.

It seems that we'll do all kinds of things in order to experience love. When we were young we teased and kicked the boy or girl we liked in order to get his or her attention. In junior high maybe you convinced a friend to see if so and so might be interested in you. In high school we souped up our faces with pimple cream and cosmetics to look as good as possible.

And while our dating habits may change as we grow older, that deep-seated need to be loved drives us to do whatever it takes to earn it. Oftentimes we feel that, in order to gain love, we have to put our best foot forward—to do what we can to impress the one whose love we want. Because we so desperately want to be loved, we'll do whatever we can to experience it.

At the same time, we not only crave love, but some of us fear it—because much of the love we've experienced over the years has been conditional or short-lived. Because we try to present ourselves in the most positive light possible we're afraid that once someone sees us for who we really are, they'll dump us or reject us. And for some of us, that's not simply a fear. We've experienced it. A marriage has fallen apart. A long relationship with a friend has ended. A father or mother abandoned us.

The thing we crave and need the most in life, love, is also the thing that can cause us the most pain in life. That's the risk of love.

The story of Easter tells us today that there is someone who can meet the deepest longings of our hearts for love and acceptance. Someone who loves us unconditionally. Someone who did something unprecedented for the sake of love, in order to win our hearts.

His name is Jesus. The Bible tells us that he loved us so much, he so desperately wanted to be our friend, that he gave his life for us on a cross to free us from anything and everything that robs us of love. He laid it on the line for us because he wanted to prove the depth of his love for us. And today we celebrate the fact that he is alive and that because he is alive we can enjoy his love every day.

Now in that extraordinary event, the death and resurrection of Jesus, we see the surprising quality of God's love—a kind of love we can't experience anywhere else.

1. God's love accepts us unconditionally. Much of the love we see and experience today is conditional. It's based on what we look like or on what we can offer the relationship. In order to gain acceptance we have to prove ourselves somehow.

But through the death and resurrection of Jesus we discover that God accepts us unconditionally. We don't have to impress him. Even though we all have our failures and shortcomings, God still believes in us, values us, and accepts us, just as we are. In other words, we don't have to earn God's love. He already loves us. Period. And he proved the extent of that love through the cross and the empty tomb.

A young couple was sitting in church one Sunday when their little boy began to seizure. Very quietly Dad picked up his son and carried him to the back of the church. And while the little boy convulsed, Dad held him firmly and lovingly, rocking him back and forth, all the while whispering words of love and encouragement to him, and never once showing any signs of embarrassment. Instead, a look of love and compassion for his son covered his face.

That's a picture of God's love for us. He loves us no matter who we are, no matter what we've done, no matter what we've been through. And even in our imperfections God lets us know that he is not embarrassed to call us his children. Instead, God lets us know that he's proud of us. God accepts us unconditionally.

2. God's love restores our dignity. There's a tribe in Africa called the Babembas. They have an effective way of dealing with people who commit a crime. Whenever a person acts irresponsibly or unjustly, he or she is placed in the center of the village alone and unbound. All work ceases as every man, woman, and child gathers around the accused. Then each person in the tribe, regardless of age, speaks to the accused, reminding him or her of all of the good things the accused has done in life. All of his or her positive attributes and actions are recounted. Not one negative word is spoken. And once everyone has shared every positive thing they can think of about the accused, the accused is welcomed back into the tribe, forgiven and accepted.

That's the way Jesus treats us. Even though we do things that hurt others, ourselves, or even God, Jesus doesn't condemn us. Instead, he reminds us that we are created in God's image. He reminds us that he believed in us enough to die and rise again so that our failures and wrongdoings might be forgiven. He reminds us that he sees beyond our shortcomings to the people we can become in him. And as we experience that kind of love and forgiveness, we find our sense of worth and value restored. Because God believes in us, we can believe in ourselves.

3. God's love stays committed to us, no matter what. One night during dinner Christy was misbehaving. Her mom warned her several times to knock it off or she'd be sent to her room. But she kept it up and sure enough, Mom made good on her word and sent Christy to bed.

After lying in bed for a few hours Christy began to feel hungry and sorry for her actions. And she started to cry. A few moments later she heard some footsteps coming toward her room. Her mom walked in, climbed into bed next to her and said, "Christy, I love you, and I've come to spend the night with you."

Because we're human we do let others down. We let ourselves down. We let God down. But God doesn't stop loving us. Instead, he stands by us and let us know that he will always remain committed to us—that he will never let us down. The cross of Jesus demonstrates the extent of that commitment. And again, there is nothing we can ever do that could ever stop God from loving us.

A young girl, sitting in church, listened as the pastor talked about the crucifixion of Jesus. As she listened, she looked up at her dad and asked, "Did Jesus really die on that cross, Daddy?" When Dad shook his head yes, his daughter said, "Well, then he can't love me now." So he turned to his daughter and said, "But honey, he can love you now, because he rose from the dead."

Deep down inside we all have the need to be loved. And we'll do some crazy things to get it. But the good news today is that you don't have to do anything to get God's love. Jesus, in the name of love, made it possible for you to enjoy God's love free of charge. He died on the cross to prove to you the extent of his love for you. And he rose again to make that love a reality to be experienced every day.

If you have not enjoyed that kind of unconditional love, I encourage you today to welcome Jesus into your life. For he promises to accept you unconditionally, to restore your worth and value, and to stay committed to you forever. And what he did for love—his death and resurrection—proves it. Let's pray together to the God who loves us.

This message was preached at an outreach-oriented Easter service by Tim Wright.

Sample Drama

You're Fine

Theme: Contentment
Thankfulness
Setting: *A psychiatrist's office. Two chairs on stage.*

Woman: Doctor, I really doubt if you can help me.

Dr.: Well, why don't you let me try.

Woman: I'm not crazy, you know.

Dr.: *(Calmly)* I'll be the judge of that. Tell me, what brings you here?

Woman: I don't know how to tell you this. . . . It's very difficult for me.

Dr.: I'm sure it is. Just think of me as a kind, listening ear.

Woman: Okay, . . . I'll try. I, uh . . . . *(Almost in tears.)* I, uh . . . don't have . . . a Mercedes.

Dr.: *(Pauses, a questioning look on his face.)* I'm not quite sure I could make out what you said. You don't have a . . .

Woman: Mercedes.

Dr.: A Mercedes? As in the vehicle? Do you not have any transportation?

Woman: No, I do . . . I have a Nissan . . . but it's not a Mercedes.

Dr.: Perhaps you can help me by sharing why this specifically upsets you so.

Woman: Doctor, my life would be better if I had a Mer . . . Mer . . . Mercedes.

Dr.: Why is it you think your life would be better?

Woman: Because Mercedes are better.

Dr.: Uh huh.

Woman: I may not have been so upset over the Mercedes if I had a . . . four-carat diamond wedding ring. *(Bursts into sobs.)*

Dr.: Are you married?

Woman: Yes.

Dr.: Do you have a wedding ring at all?

Woman: Yes. *(Looks at it.)* But it's not four carats. SEE!

Dr.: Well . . .

Woman: We don't have a Jacuzzi, either.

Dr.: No? *(Getting caught up in her emotions.)*

Woman: No. And you know what else?

Dr.: What?

Woman: My home is just a three-bedroom, with one and a half baths. I wanted a four-bedroom with two and three-quarter baths. And we just have a two-car garage. I always hoped I'd have that extra garage space.

Dr.: *(Broken up along with her.)* For the Mercedes? *(Both start sobbing. Suddenly the doctor stops.)* Wait a minute. Why am I crying? You shouldn't be crying either, really.

Woman: I could scream—that would be better.

Dr.: Life can't be about bigger and better. I don't think there's anything too wrong here. You're fine.

Woman: But you've heard all that I don't have.

Dr.: Well, more than that, I've heard all that you do have. And that's really what we need to be dealing with.

Woman: I am aware of what I have. It's just that what I have isn't what I thought I'd have.

Dr.: And what is it that you thought you'd have.

Woman: Well, everything that I've listed. And more.

Dr.: More?

Woman: Not just things. Just, more life, I guess. You know, I was one of the ones who thought that I would have it all. I expected nothing less. I'll tell you, it's a big disappointment to see where I've actually ended up. And then you're thinking, this is all there is?

Dr.: Well, I see. One question. Is all there is really all that bad?

Woman: Hmm . . . I never really thought much about what I do have. I've always looked at how much I missed the mark.

Dr.: Whose mark is that?

Woman: Mine. The one I set for myself.

Dr.: I think maybe you've focused long enough on the mark you say you've missed. Since all you have is all there is right now, let's start there. You're fine.

Sample Reader's Theater

The Rib

Theme: Marriage

Setting: *Two music stands or podiums across the stage from each other. Each speaker stands behind the music stand and reads the script.*

Eve: He calls me, Honey.

Adam: Hey, Honey?

Eve: I call him, Sugar. Just a minute, Sugar! Honey . . . Sugar . . . sounds like a good recipe for rib sauce.

Adam: (*Uncomfortable look, thinking he heard "that word."*) Honey, what did you say?

Eve: Oops, that word makes him nervous. He thinks he'll have to go into surgery again. Not that he regrets the surgery. I mean, there weren't any complications or anything. He had the best surgeon he could get. The best anesthesiologist, for that matter. It's just that "missin' the rib" thing that makes him a little queasy. But hey, he has me, what's one less rib?

Adam: (*Nervously*) Honey, did you say something?

Eve: I better keep it down. It's just that I don't often get the opportunity to talk about, well, you know. (*Mouths.*) T-H-E R-I-B. But it is kind of the way we met. Kind of the reason we're together.

Adam: I love you, Honey.

Eve: I love you, too, Sugar. And it's really, when you think about it, a big help in keeping a close-knit marriage. If I think about how we were introduced, T-H-E R-I-B, it starts to make a lot of sense. We were like, "linked together" intentionally. We were meant to work together. If we focus on the fact that there was and is a master plan for marriage, it gives us a sense of security that it's not in vain. We've had our difficult times, you know. The apple thing was a big one, but just knowing that the rib was on purpose . . .

Adam: (*Nervously*) Honey?

Eve: . . . makes a close-knit marriage seem a little more . . . a lot more possible. I'm coming, Sugar!

Contemporary Performance Songs
(Music Available)

Easter
"A Wondrous Exchange" (P/S)

Artist: Luke Garrett

Ever Constant Ever Sure

Words and Music: Dwight Liles/Luke Garrett/Niles Borop

Copyright © 1987 Bug and Bear Music

Family/Children
"Above All Else" (P/S)

Artist: Debby Boone

Friends for Life

Words and Music: Michael and Stormie Omartian

Copyright © 1987 See This House Music

Praise
"Almighty" (P/MF)

Artist: Wayne Watson

Home Free

Words and Music: Wayne Watson

Copyright © 1990 Word Music

Christmas/Easter
"Amen" (P/M)

Artist: Larnelle Harris

I've Just Seen Jesus

Words and Music: Traditional

Copyright © 1981 Paragon Music Corp.

Christian Living
"Basics of Life (The)" (P/MF)

Artist: 4Him

The Basics of Life

Words and Music: Mark Harris

Copyright © 1992 Paragon Music Corp.

Grace
"Be Ye Glad" (P/S)

Artist: Debby Boone

Friends for Life

Words and Music: Michael Kelly Blanchard

Copyright © 1980 Paragon Music Corp.

Praise
"Bless Ye the Lord" (P/F)

Artist: First Call

First Call Studio Collection

Words and Music: Dan Keen/Justin Peters

Copyright © 1984 Meadowgreen Music Co.

Family
"Built on Amazing Grace" (P/M)

Artist: 4Him

The Basics of Life

Words and Music: Mark Harris/Don Koch

Copyright © 1992 Paragon Music Corp.

Friendship
"Can You Reach My Friend" (P/S)
Artist: Debby Boone
Surrender
Words and Music: Billy Sprague/Jim Weber
Copyright © 1983 Meadowgreen Music

Opener
"Celebrate" (P/F)
Artist: Wayne Watson
Man in the Middle
Words and Music: Randy Lanson
Copyright © 1984 Straightway Music

Christmas
"Celebrate the Child" (P/MF)
Artist: Michael Card
The Final Word
Words and Music: Michael Card
Copyright © 1986 Mole End Music/Birdwing Music

Faith
"Consider It Done" (P/MF)
Artist: Steven Curtis Chapman
Steven Curtis Chapman Songbook
Words and Music: Steven Curtis Chapman
Copyright © 1988 Sparrow Song

Mission
"Do They Know" (P/S)
Artist: Steven Curtis Chapman
Steven Curtis Chapman Songbook
Words and Music: Steven Curtis Chapman
Copyright © 1987 Life Song Music Press

Love
"Do You Believe in Love" (P/M)
Artist: Michael English
Michael English
Words and Music: Chris Eaton
Copyright © 1985 Patch Music LTD

Faith
"Don't Let the Fire Die" (P/MS)
Artist: Steven Curtis Chapman
The Great Adventure
Words and Music: Steven Curtis Chapman
Copyright © 1992 Sparrow Song

Love
"Don't Throw Away the Love" (P/S)
Artist: Dick and Mel Tunney
Let the Dreamers Dream
Words and Music: Dick and Mel Tunney
Copyright © 1991 BMG Songs, Inc.

Opener/Truth
"Facts Are Facts" (R/F)
Artist: Steven Curtis Chapman
Heaven in a Real World
Words and Music: Steven Curtis Chapman
Copyright © 1994 Sparrow Song/Peach Hill Songs

Faithfulness
"Faithful Too" (P/MF)
Artist: Steven Curtis Chapman
Steven Curtis Chapman Songbook
Words and Music: Steven Curtis Chapman/Geoff Moore
Copyright © 1988 Sparrow Song

Hurt
"Find a Hurt and Heal It" (P/MF)
Artist: Debby Boone
Surrender
Words and Music: David Baroni/Niles Borop
Copyright © 1984 Word Music

Stress
"Forever in His Care" (J/S)
Artist: First Call
First Call Studio Collection
Words and Music: Randal Dennis
Copyright © 1987 Birdwing Music

Faith
"Freedom" (P/MF)

Artist: First Call

The First Call Vocal Collection

Words and Music: David Batteau/Darrell Brown/
    Marabeth Jordon

Copyright © 1993 Birdwing Music

Missions
"Freedom" (PR/F)

Artist: Wayne Watson

Home Free

Words and Music: Wayne Watson

Copyright © 1990 Word Music

Comfort
"Friend of a Wounded Heart" (P/S)

Artist: Wayne Watson

Watercolor Ponies

Words and Music: Claire Cloninger/Wayne Watson

Copyright © 1987 Word Music

Christmas
"Gloria" (PR/F)

Artist: Whiteheart

A Home Sweet Home Christmas

Words and Music: Billy Smiley/Mark Gersmehl

Copyright © 1984 Bug and Bear Music

Family/Marriage
"Go There with You" (P/M)

Artist: Steven Curtis Chapman

The Great Adventure

Words and Music: Steven Curtis Chapman

Copyright © 1992 Sparrow Song

Hope
"God Is Greater" (P/S)

Artist: First Call

First Call Studio Collection

Words and Music: Greg Fisher/Greg Davis

Copyright © 1986 Life Song Music Press

Opener
"Great Adventure (The)" (PR/F)

Artist: Steven Curtis Chapman

The Great Adventure

Words and Music: Steven Curtis Chapman/Geoff
    Moore

Copyright © 1992 Sparrow Song

Grace
"He'll Do Whatever It Takes" (P/MS)

Artist: Phillips, Craig and Dean

Lifeline

Words and Music: Dan Dean

Copyright © 1994 Dawn Treader Music

Commitment
"Heart's Cry" (P/S)

Artist: Steven Curtis Chapman

The Great Adventure

Words and Music: Steven Curtis Chapman/Phil
    Naish

Copyright © 1992 Sparrow Song

Compassion
"Helping Hand" (P/M)

Artist: Amy Grant

House of Love

Words and Music: Tommy Sills/Amy Grant/Beverly
    Damall

Copyright © 1994 Bases Loaded Music/Age to Age
    Music, Inc.

Stress
"Hiding Place" (P/S)

Artist: Steven Curtis Chapman

Steven Curtis Chapman Songbook

Words and Music: Steven Curtis Chapman/Jerry
    Salley

Copyright © 1987 Sparrow Song

Opener
"His Love Is Strong" (P/F)
Artist: Clay Crosse
Clay Crosse—Time to Believe
Words and Music: Regie Hamm/Joe Lindsey
Copyright © 1994 Paragon Music

Christian Living
"The Human Race" (P/MF)
Artist: Steven Curtis Chapman
Steven Curtis Chapman Songbook
Words and Music: Steven Curtis Chapman
Copyright © 1988 Sparrow Song/New Wings
  Music

Belonging
"I Found Myself in You" (P/M)
Artist: Clay Crosse
Clay Crosse—Time to Believe
Words and Music: Ellis Hall/Jud Friedman
Copyright © 1988 Warner-Tamerlane Publishing

Christmas
"I Have Held My King" (P/S)
Artist: Glen Allen Green
A Home Sweet Home Christmas
Words and Music: Glen Allen Green/Keith Thomas
Copyright © 1985 Word Music/Bug and Bear
  Music

Family/Parenting
"I Want to Be Just Like You" (CP/M)
Artist: Phillips, Craig and Dean
Lifeline
Words and Music: Dan Dean
Copyright © 1994 PraiseSong Press

Commitment
"I Want to Be Where You Are" (P/S)
Choral piece
God with Us

Words and Music: Don Moen
Copyright © 1989/1992 Integrity's Hosanna!
  Music

God's Promises
"I've Got a Right" (P/F)
Artist: Babbie Mason
With All My Heart
Words and Music: Babbie Mason/Donna Douglas
Copyright © 1990 Word Music

Christmas
"Immanuel" (P/M)
Artist: Michael Card
The Promise
Words and Music: Michael Card
Copyright © 1991 Birdwing Music/Mole End
  Music

Faith
"In Christ Alone" (P/S)
Artist: Michael English
Michael English
Words and Music: Shawn Craig/Don Koch
Copyright © 1990 Paragon Music Corp.

Christmas
"Joseph's Song" (P/S)
Artist: Michael Card
The Promise
Words and Music: Michael Card
Copyright © 1982 Whole Armor Publishing Co.

Loving God
"Just Can't Help Myself" (P/MF)
Artist: First Call
The First Call Vocal Collection
Words and Music: Joe Hogue/Marabeth Jordon/
  Paul Salveson
Copyright © 1993 Careers-BMG Music Publish-
  ing, Inc.

Family/Marriage
"Just Never Say It Enough" (P/S)

Artist: Wayne Watson
Home Free
Words and Music: Wayne Watson
Copyright © 1990 Word Music

Stress
"Keep Rollin' On" (CP/F)

Artist: Debby Boone
Surrender
Words and Music: Harry Browning
Copyright © 1982 Paragon Music

Praise
"Lord of All" (P/MS)

Artist: First Call
First Call Studio Collection
Words and Music: Phil McHugh
Copyright © 1987 River Oaks Music Co.

Easter
"Love Found a Way" (P/M)

Artist: Wayne Watson
Man in the Middle
Words and Music: Greg Nelson/Phil McHugh
Copyright © 1982 River Oaks Music Co.

Rejuvenation
"Love from the Sweetest Cup" (P/MF)

Artist: Clay Crosse
Clay Crosse—Time to Believe
Words and Music: Arnie Roman/Russ Desalvo/
  Terry Cox
Copyright © 1995 Romanesque Music WNR
  Group Music

Commitment
"Love You with My Life" (P/MF)

Artist: Steven Curtis Chapman
More to This Life
Words and Music: Steven Curtis Chapman
Copyright © 1989 Sparrow Song/New Wings

Christmas
"Mary Did You Know" (P/S)

Artist: Michael English
Michael English
Words and Music: Mark Lowry/Buddy Greene
Copyright © 1991 Word Music

Money
"Material Magic" (P/M)

Artist: Wayne Watson
Watercolor Ponies
Words and Music: Wayne Watson
Copyright © 1987 Word Music

Praise
"Messiah" (PR/F)

Artist: First Call
First Call Studio Collection
Words and Music: Mark Baldwin/John Elliot
Copyright © 1984 Laurel Press

Prayer
"Midnight Oil" (P/S)

Artist: Phillips, Craig, and Dean
Lifeline
Words and Music: Joy Becker and Shawn Craig
Copyright © 1992 Ariose Music/PraiseSong
  Press

Faith
"My God" (P/MS)

Artist: Luke Garrett
Ever Constant Ever Sure
Words and Music: Chris Christian
Copyright © 1987 Home Sweet Home Music

God's Faithfulness
"My Redeemer Is Faithful and True" (P/S)

Artist: Steven Curtis Chapman

Steven Curtis Chapman Songbook
Words and Music: Steven Curtis Chapman/James Isaac Elliott
Copyright © 1987 Sparrow Song

Opener
"My Turn Now" (P/MF)
Artist: Steven Curtis Chapman
Steven Curtis Chapman Songbook
Words and Music: Steven Curtis Chapman/Brent Lamb
Copyright © 1988 Sparrow Song/New Wings Music

Opener
"No Better Place" (PR/F)
Artist: Steven Curtis Chapman
For the Sake of the Call
Words and Music: Steven Curtis Chapman/Phil Naish
Copyright © 1990 Sparrow Song

Intimacy with God
"No One Knows My Heart" (P/S)
Artist: Susan Ashton
Wakened by the Wind
Words and Music: Susan Ashton/Billy Sprague/ Wayne Kirkpatrick
Copyright © 1991 Birdwing Music

Crucifixion
"O Calvary's Lamb" (P/S)
Artist: Sandi Patti
Another Time, Another Place
Words and Music: Chaz Bosarge/Bill George/ Tommy Greer
Copyright © 1989 Word Music

Crucifixion
"Only the Hands" (P/S)
Artist: NewSong
Living Proof
Words and Music: Eddie Carswell/Steven Curtis

Chapman/Olive
Copyright © 1990 Dayspring Music

Future
"Over the Horizon" (J/MF)
Artist: 4Him
4Him Songbook
Words and Music: Mark Harris/Don Koch/Dave Clark
Copyright © 1991 First Verse Music

God's Love
"Rose Colored Glasses" (P/S)
Artist: Wayne Watson
Watercolor Ponies
Words and Music: Wayne Watson
Copyright © 1987 Word Music

Christian Living
"Run Away" (P/MF)
Artist: Steven Curtis Chapman
Steven Curtis Chapman Songbook
Words and Music: Steven Curtis Chapman
Copyright © 1987 Sparrow Song

Family/Marriage
"Said and Done" (P/MF)
Artist: Steven Curtis Chapman
Steven Curtis Chapman Songbook
Words and Music: Steven Curtis Chapman
Copyright © 1987 Sparrow Song

Faith
"Solid as the Rock" (R/F)
Artist: Michael English
Michael English
Words and Music: Larry Bryant/Geoff Thurman
Copyright © 1989 Stonebrook Music Co.

Faith
"Step of Faith" (J/MF)
Artist: First Call
First Call Studio Collection

Words and Music: Melodie Tunney/Dick Tunney/
  Niles Borop
Copyright © 1988 Word Music

Family/Teenagers
"Teenager in the House"
(PR/F)
Artist: Wayne Watson
Home Free
Words and Music: Wayne Watson
Copyright © 1990 Material Music/Word Music

Hope
"That's Paradise" (PR/M)
Artist: Steven Curtis Chapman
The Great Adventure
Words and Music: Steven Curtis Chapman/Geoff
  Moore
Copyright © 1992 Sparrow Song

Love
"That's What Love Is For"
(P/M)
Artist: Amy Grant
Heart in Motion
Words and Music: Michael Omartian/Mark
  Muller/Amy Grant
Copyright © 1991 All Nations Music

God's Name
"The Name Above All
Names" (P/MS)
Artist: Debby Boone
Friends for Life
Words and Music: Chuck Girard
Copyright © 1982 Sea of Glass Music

Praise
"The Reason We Sing" (P/MS)
Artist: First Call
First Call Studio Collection
Words and Music: Dick and Melodie Tunney
Copyright © 1988 LCS Songs

Grace
"The Time Is Now" (P/MF)
Artist: Debby Boone
Friends for Life
Words and Music: Michael and Stormie Omartian
Copyright © 1984 See This House

Easter
"Today Is the Day" (P/F)
Artist: David Meece
"7" and Songs from "Count the Cost"
Words and Music: David Meece
Copyright © 1983/1985 Meece Music

Opener/Worth
"Treasure of You" (P/F)
Artist: Steven Curtis Chapman
Heaven in the Real World
Words and Music: Steven Curtis Chapman/Geoff
  Moore
Copyright © 1994 Sparrow Song/Peach Hill Songs/
  Starstruck Music

Grace
"Tuesday's Child" (P/MF)
Artist: Steven Curtis Chapman
Steven Curtis Chapman Songbook
Words and Music: Steven Curtis Chapman/Dale
  Oliver/Dave Mull
Copyright © 1988 Sparrow Song

Love
"Unconditional Love" (P/S)
Artist: Debby Boone
Friends for Life
Words and Music: Randy Goodrum
Copyright © 1987 California Phase Music

Unity
"Undivided" (P/M)
Artist: First Call
First Call Studio Collection
Words and Music: Melodie Tunney

Copyright © 1985 Laurel Press

Faith
"Walk in the Dark" (P/F)
Artist: Wayne Watson
A Beautiful Place
Words and Music: Wayne Watson
Copyright © 1993 Word Music

Prayer
"When God's People Pray"
(P/MS)
Artist: Wayne Watson
Home Free
Words and Music: Wayne Watson
Copyright © 1990 Word Music

Christian Living
"When I Am Gone" (P/MS)
Artist: 4Him
4Him Songbook
Words and Music: Mark Harris/Don Koch/Dave
    Clark
Copyright © 1990 First Verse Music

Friendship
"When You Are a Soldier"
(P/MS)
Artist: Steven Curtis Chapman
For the Sake of the Call
Words and Music: Steven Curtis Chapman
Copyright © 1990 Sparrow Song

Faith
"Where There Is Faith"
(P/MS)
Artist: 4Him
4Him Songbook
Words and Music: Billy Simon
Copyright © 1992 River Oaks Music Co.

Faith
"Why" (P/M)
Artist: 4Him
4Him Songbook
Words and Music: Mark Harris/Don Koch/Dave
    Clark
Copyright © 1991 First Verse Music

Commitment
"Would I Know You Now"
(P/S)
Artist: Wayne Watson
Watercolor Ponies
Words and Music: Wayne Watson
Copyright © 1987 Word Music

Christian Living
"You Know Better" (P/MF)
Artist: Steven Curtis Chapman
For the Sake of the Call
Words and Music: Steven Curtis Chapman
Copyright © 1990 Sparrow Song

Contemporary Performance Songs
(No Music Available)

Commitment
"As Long as My Heart Knows It's You" (P/M)

4Him—The Ride
Words and Music: Dave Clark/Mark Harris/Don Koch
Copyright © 1994 Word Music

Prayer
"Between You and Me" (P/MS)

4Him—The Ride
Words and Music: Mark Harris/Don Koch/Peter Wolf
Copyright © 1994 Paragon Music Corp.

Grace
"Extra Measure" (CP/M)

Paul Smith—Extra Measure
Words and Music: Jeff Silvey/Paul Smith
Copyright © 1993 Sparrow Music

Trust
"Fearless Heart" (P/M)

East to West
Words and Music: Susan Gaither Jennings/Don Koch
Copyright © 1993 Townsend & Warbucks Music

Prayer
"He Is There" (P/MF)

East to West
Words and Music: Jay DeMarcus/Brian White
Copyright © 1993 LifeSong Music

Support
"Holy Hand" (P/F)

Morgan Cryar—Like a River
Words and Music: Morgan Cryar
Copyright © 1989 Edward Grant, Inc.

Truth
"Hungry for You" (P/F)

East to West
Words and Music: Ty Lacy/Dennis Patton/Steve Siler
Copyright © 1993 Ariose Music

Security
"I Know Where I Stand" (CP/MS)

Sometimes Miracles Hide
Words and Music: Bruce Carroll/Claire Coninger
Copyright © 1991 Word Music

Crucifixion
"I'll Take the Cross" (P/S)

Allison Durham—Walk into Freedom
Words and Music: Dawn Thomas
Copyright © 1993 Magnolia Hill Music

Life with Christ
"It's a Wonderful Life" (PR/F)

All Around the World
Words and Music: Eddie Carswell/Leonard Ahlstrom
Copyright © 1993 LifeSong Music Press

Love
"Love Never Looked Like This" (P/M)
Allison Durham—Walk into Freedom
Words and Music: Geoff Thurman/Michael Puryear/
Dave Clark
Copyright © 1993 Meadowgreen Music

Support
"Name Above All Names" (P/MF)
Morgan Cryar—Like a River
Words and Music: Morgan Cryar
Copyright © 1993 Edward Grant, Inc.

Missions
"Not Too Far from Here" (P/S)
Kim Boyce—By Faith
Words and Music: Ty Lacy/Steve Siler
Copyright © 1993 Shepherd's Fold Music BMI/
Ariose Music

Missions
"Real Thing" (P/MF)
4Him—The Ride
Words and Music: Dave Clark/Mark Harris/Don
Koch
Copyright © 1994 Word Music

Priorities
"Unimportant Things" (P/S)
Paul Smith—Extra Measure
Words and Music: Geoff Thurman/Lowell Alexander
Copyright © Meadowgreen Music/ASCAP

Opener
"Welcome to the Next Level" (P/F)
East to West
Words and Music: Todd Burns/Brian White
Copyright © 1993 Paragon Music Corp.

Faith
"Where Faith Belongs" (P/M)
Paul Smith—Extra Measure
Words and Music: B. Carroll/J. Adams/G. Garner/
P. Smith
Copyright © Word Music/ASCAP